# WHITE MAN, YELLOW MAN

# WHITE MAN, YELLOW MAN

## Two Novellas

### Shusaku Endo
TRANSLATED BY Teruyo Shimizu

Paulist Press
New York / Mahwah, NJ

Cover image by Irina_QQQ/Shutterstock.com
Cover design by Sharyn Banks
Book design by Lynn Else

Library of Congress Cataloging-in-Publication Data
Endo, Shusaku, 1923-1996.
    [Shiroi hito. English]
    White Man, Yellow Man : two novellas / Shusaku Endo ; translated by Teruyo Shimizu.
        pages cm
    ISBN 978-0-8091-4862-2 (alk. paper) — ISBN 978-1-58768-370-1
    I. Shimizu, Teruyo, 1967- translator. II. Title.
    PL849.N4S4913 2014
    895.6`35—dc23

                                                        2013042429


ISBN 978-0-8091-4862-2 (paperback)
ISBN 978-1-58768-370-1 (e-book)

Published by Paulist Press
997 Macarthur Boulevard
Mahwah, New Jersey 07430

www.paulistpress.com

Printed and bound in the
United States of America

# WHITE MAN

# Chapter I

January 28, 1942. I am going to make a record of this. The Allies are already advancing on Valence. They will arrive in Lyon as early as tomorrow or the day after tomorrow. The Nazis know best that they are bound to be defeated.

At this very moment, as I write this note, the windows of my room are violently shaking. Not due to the artillery fire from the Resistance, but to the explosion the Nazis themselves just set off on the bridge over the Rhone. No matter what the Nazis try, however—destroying the bridges, or cutting off Route K2, which connects Vienne to Lyon— it is simply impossible to stop the surging tidal wave of Allied troops. They say General von Stadt in Paris ordered his men to defend Lyon to the death. But I don't know if they could pull off even a retreating maneuver, let alone a defense of Lyon to the death.

Every face is bestial. Since yesterday, the Nazis' hatred of the Allies has been redirected against the residents of Lyon. Just as cornered rats will attack one another instead of their natural enemy, the cat, so the Nazi soldiers—Franz, Hans, Peter, and the rest—pour into Lyon merely to torment its citizens. In Republique Street, in Emile Zola Street, they rape girls and vandalize houses and stores. So much for the vaunted military discipline of the Nazis.

I can't help sneering, just thinking of their bloody eyes, their faces twisted in indignation. Culture, Christianity, Humanism—these are all good for nothing today. And I

3

don't think this is so only with the Nazis. The same goes for all men—the Allied troops, the civilized Europeans, the Yellow races, whatever. The people who are massacred today will be slaughterers and torturers tomorrow. Yes, tomorrow will be the day when the snarling citizens of Lyon lash out at any Germans delinquent in escaping, and at the collaborators who betrayed them. The Marquis de Sade put it well:

> ...so human blood is tinted red
> And human eyes glitter with the pleasure of
> torturing

As I close my eyes, I can clearly remember the whiteness of the maid Yvonne's fleshy thighs as she pinned down that old dog. I think that is the true stance human beings take toward one another.

Yvonne's white thighs...

From the window of our house in the Croix Rousse I watched as the scene transpired out in the street, where wisteria flowers were falling, and it left a critical scar on my boyhood. But why did that scene impress itself on my mind, as with a burning seal, when other boys would have overlooked it as nothing? I think it is necessary to follow that memory back into my childhood in order to explain what later made me, a Frenchman, choose to collaborate with the Gestapo, and to torture my fellow countrymen.

My father was French. He became engaged to my German mother while he was at a technical school in Lille. After marrying, they settled in Lyon. I was an ugly boy, and what's more, was born cross-eyed. When I try to remember

4

my father's face, I always think of those vulgar portraits of eighteenth-century libertines. I mean the faces in those clumsy, obscene drawings the old women sold next to the Opera House in Lyon, together with dirty magazines. In truth, my father was short and fleshy—indeed, he was a little fat. He had flabby, white flesh, and the small hands of a woman. His eyes were always moist, perhaps because his lachrymal glands had developed excessively. He had never suffered a serious illness, had never experienced the terror of death, when he was killed in a car accident some time later.

I have poked my finger onto his rubber-ball flesh. The impression would remain on his skin for a long time. And come to think of it now, it might well have been hatred of the man's debauchery that drove my mother into her strict Puritanism. The man who cared only about pleasure had no love left for his skinny cross-eyed son. There is one incident that I can never forget. "To the right. I'm telling you to look to the RIGHT," my father said one day, moving his finger in front of my eyes. Then he purposely heaved a big sigh. "You won't be popular with the girls. Never."

Not until that moment had I been made to understand clearly just how ugly I was. I hated my father for being cruel enough to tell me that to my face. It became unbearable for me to look in the mirror, to pass a girl on the street, or to be introduced to a new maid.

I don't know how much my father loved my mother. He was kept away from home half of each month by what he called business. There was another incident, which occurred when I was eleven, as I recall. Mother wasn't home that day. And father brought a young woman with nut-brown hair back from the factory. They shut themselves up in a room for quite a while. As the woman left, she petted me on the head

5

and said, "Cute boy." I hated her at once. She pulled a bag of bonbons from her purse and gave it to me.

I didn't tell my mother about the woman or the bonbons. Certainly it was not because I took my father's side, or because I felt sorry for my mother. No, somehow I simply took pleasure in concealing the secret *as a secret*. I savored the sweet taste of that secret at leisure, as I nibbled the bonbons in bed, alone. But I don't want anybody to misunderstand. My atheism has nothing to do with the way my father disciplined me. It would be more accurate to say it sprang up in resistance to the pious Puritanism of my mother.

It is hard to imagine what it was like to be a Protestant family in Lyon in the 1930s. As a natural reaction against my father, my mother forced on me a very strict asceticism. After I reached ten years of age, she would not permit me to sit alone even with my female cousin. She dreaded my sexual awakening more than anything, as she believed it would tempt me to sin. She insisted I avert my eyes from my lower body when I changed into pajamas, and forbade me to put my hands under the blanket. She was desperate to eliminate anything that might fuel the fire in my body, where the flames of desire were, in truth, already hardly negligible.

*Poor naive mother!*—I often thought, years later. She needn't have troubled herself so, because I knew well that my appearance would be an object of ridicule for girls. And she had forgotten the old proverb: "Stamping on a fire only feeds the flames." Anyway, my mother saw to it that I was not going to read anything other than the books the priests at the Protestant elementary school in Saint Irénée gave us. She must have thought that even books like *Cendrillon* or *Arabian Nights*, popular among children my age, would stimulate my sensuality, as she never permitted me even to borrow them from friends.

The Lyon of the 1930s wasn't very different from the Lyon of the eighteenth century. In our old, damp house in the Croix Rousse, where the odor of human beings had accumulated over many decades, I just existed quietly all alone doing nothing. Unlike other boys, I couldn't even play "house," or play quoits with the girls. But the devil's greatest stratagem is never to show himself clearly. And one day, quite abruptly, he taught the pleasure of evil to me, who was supposed to have been protected from every sin.

There was an old stray dog around my house. It used to belong to an old shoemaker, and after the man died from consumption, the dog would not leave the house, and roamed around the neighborhood, day after day. I greatly feared meeting up with this dog on my way to and from school. He had lost some of his hair, perhaps due to some kind of skin disease, exposing his red flesh. Besides that, he was always coughing, just like his old owner. I was gnawed by the anxiety that I might catch tuberculosis from it, if not skin disease.

It was toward the end of the spring. I was twelve. I was sick that day and hadn't gone to school. So mother made me stay in bed upstairs. She was down in the living room talking to the priest, who happened to stop by. It was quiet.

As I lay, I gazed outside, bored. My bed stood alongside the window, and, if I leaned a little toward it, I could see the street in front.

It was midday. Nobody was about. Wisteria grew along a tall fence on the other side of the street. The wind was scattering its purple petals on the ground.

But then...I saw a queer scene. Yvonne, our maid, was squatting down at the edge of the street, beckoning at something with her hand. And now and then she shook a piece of meat, which she gripped in her other hand. I began to wonder what she was up to.

The sick old dog staggered toward Yvonne, coughing all the way. He hung his head down between Yvonne's legs, as if imploring her.

All at once Yvonne grabbed a length of cord. Pinning the dog's head down with one knee as he struggled to escape, Yvonne deftly bound the cord around its muzzle. I watched the scene unfold, leaning my upper body against the window, trembling. Slowly Yvonne raised the meat tantalizingly to the dog's mouth, which he could no longer open. The dog tried to retreat, cramping his legs, and Yvonne started beating it fiercely. His head pinned down by the maid's fat white thigh, the dog could only suffer, kicking at the ground in vain. At length, Yvonne raised her knee and untied the cord. Then she made her way to the entrance to our house, looking as if nothing had happened.

To this day, I don't know why the old maid did it. Maybe she was getting her revenge on the dog for having filched a piece of meat from the kitchen. Whatever the reason, the scene had a conclusive effect on the life of the twelve-year-old boy who peeked out of that window. I saw all, quivering, and not because I was horrified. No, it was because, on that day, the forbidding wall of Puritanism that a poor mother had built around her son came crashing down. What I experienced was the pleasure of lust. Yvonne's fleshy thigh, the thigh that pinned the old, consumptive dog down, remained in my eyes, always white, an incandescent white. And so my sexual awakening was accompanied by the pleasure of abuse.

I was neither foolish nor innocent enough to tell my dark secret to others. I'm sure my father, my mother, the priest at school—all of them remained convinced I was a boy free from evil pleasures.

In the chapel, I feigned sincerity in my prayers, conforming to the image that had been presented to me. But it was never God that I gazed up at in the chapel of the John Calvin Grammar School in Saint Irénée. What attracted me was the depiction of hell hanging on the wall. The damned were naked, and black devils were torturing them. Some were lashed, while others had their arms or legs torn off. What once terrified me now stimulated a palpable pleasure. I recognized in the devil's wide eyes the inexplicable bliss I first experienced that day.

I still wonder today why that feeling didn't arise in other children, why only in me. The Freudians say that some sort of complex toward one's mother feeds and cultivates a sadism like mine. Suppose they are right. Somewhere in my mind I might have hated my mother for disciplining me so thoroughly, denying me pleasure and freedom, and confining me to my room in the Croix Rousse throughout my childhood. And that hatred might have grown into a detestation of women in general. But I feel I must make a point. Sadism, in my case, doesn't lend itself to this sort of convenient psychoanalytic diagnosis. I didn't feel abusive simply toward women. Later, I started to feel a desire to torment not only women, but *everyone*—indeed, to use somewhat grandiloquent terms, all of mankind.

But I have to hurry. I haven't much time left. An intense explosion is shaking the window again, and dust is falling from the walls and ceiling. It must be the Lafayette Bridge going up now.

No, I really don't care about all this. It's none of my business if the Nazis are put to rout, or if the Allies recapture Lyon, or if "fascism" collapses and what they call "democracy" wins. The French Resistance, the Communists, and the Christians may all hope to see some historical progress, some proof of justice at work, in this series of events. But as for me, I'm utterly indifferent.

If there is anything in the fate of Lyon the day after tomorrow that concerns me at all, it will be my denunciation as a traitor who cooperated with the Gestapo. My fellow citizens will take their revenge on me for having been one of the conspirators of the "Pomme de Pin" incident, during which the marquis and his men were racked and abused. I'm going to escape, no doubt. I must live. History can never annihilate me, can never annihilate the torturer in me. It is a fact. And I want to record that fact in this diary.

# Chapter II

No one uncovered my dark secret. To be sure, I don't imagine that my mother, my teachers, or the priest ever thought of me as quite an angel. But they regarded me as simply a skinny, pale, diligent boy. Had they been fooled? Not really. The flame of sexual desire that the scene of Yvonne and the old dog ignited at the foundation of my existence remained buried, if only temporarily, under the ashes. I tried to conform myself to the image of me that the adults with whom I was surrounded all entertained, and before I noticed, I myself had forgotten about the incident.

Physically, I developed more slowly than the other boys. When I entered Henri IV Secondary School, which sits behind the Opera in Lyon, my friends there liked to chat about female students, or about the prostitutes in Gallieni Street. But I was hardly interested in that sort of talk. I knew all too well that I wasn't attractive. And I can report that I was utterly free from the "playboy" fever most boys my age would have caught, at least once. Still, occasionally, I felt my body tremble as I looked out of the window at twilight on a spring day onto the lonely street where wisteria petals were falling, just as I had done on that day when I was twelve. In my mind, my hands underwent spasms of desire to torture something, I knew not what. It took real effort to drive away the illusion, and my pajamas and sheets were soaked with sweat.

Once, the summer before I graduated from Henri IV Secondary School, my father took me on a trip to Aden, in

11

Arabia, which was unusual. It was a business trip. He needed to buy some flax for his factory. But the trip, that day of it in particular, would come to mean something else to me.

What incited me to do what I did that one day might have been the sense of freedom I felt in the desert of southeast Arabia, far away from conventional, ponderous Lyon, where ethics, religion, family, and school all bound in human instincts and desires. Or it might simply have been the maddening August heat coming in off the Red Sea.

Our ship arrived in Aden in mid-August. We stayed at the England Hotel, the only European-style lodging in the city. My father caroused all day with men from the branch office of the company he had come to do business with, and I was left alone. My mother couldn't oversee me, nor could the priest restrain me. I was free and could do anything I wanted.

In the intense heat, sufficient to make me dizzy, I relished at leisure a sense of freedom granted me for the first time in my life. I walked around by myself in the maze of white streets, where black Africans, brown Arabs, and women with faces wrapped in black cloth wriggled. Wherever you stood in the city, you could see the glittering blue ocean, and the terraced salt fields along it, which looked like castles. The sun was an incandescent ball, always hovering above a bare mountain behind the city. The color of the sky was gloomy and leaden.

I witnessed a stunt in the streets thronged with natives. The performers were an Arabian girl, barely clothed, and a boy. The girl's body looked slimy, gleaming with sweat and grease. She danced, turning and twisting her silver, snake-like arms and legs. The audience consisted of no more than

12

several men. They watched as she danced, their bony legs crossed, eating baked treats.

All of a sudden, the girl made the boy lie down on the ground. His legs bent up in a curve, little by little, until they reached the back of his head. The posture reminded me of a scorpion at the moment of mating. Then the girl leapt onto his legs and head, and the boy's body bent unbearably.

"Eeeeek!"

Surely he had let out a groan of pain from his tightly clenched lips. But the girl showed no mercy. She started to march in place, on his head. Her black eyes became narrow and long, and a flame of cruelty burned inside them.

I almost fainted. The sun still sat above the bare mountain, glaring and fixed, behind the city of Aden. The air grew more and more inflamed under the heavy, lead-colored sky, almost paralyzing my body. I ran like a madman to our hotel.

My father was planning to go to Port Said the next day, and, of course, he suggested that I go and see this, the biggest port in Egypt, with him. But I declined. I had to make good use of my father's absence and visit that maze of streets again.

It was already noon. I changed into a patterned dress shirt. Into my pocket I put the money my father had given me to buy lunch, and made my way back to the scene of that performance.

The boy was there, the same as yesterday, but he had transformed himself into a beggar, asking alms from passersby. In broken English, he offered to show me around Aden.

The two of us set out. He walked in front, lagged behind, and occasionally spoke to me in unintelligible English. The sun was still there, fixed and incandescent, and as oppressive as ever. Suddenly the boy began to shout, "Nice girl!"

13

It seemed he intended to take me to the Arabian girl I had seen yesterday. I shook my head in a sulk. We stopped as we came near the salt fields, both of us soaked with sweat. I took off my shirt and went half naked. Noticing the thick, brown wall of rock rising eerily in front of me, exuding salt, for the first time I pulled out my money.

The high rock ahead of us was of a loud, primary color. It stood among dry grasses, which had been burnt by waves of heat. I walked on with my wet shirt in my right hand. The boy followed in silence. The rock cast a totally black shadow behind it. We paused. My neck and chest were washed by sweat and felt sticky.

I whispered to the boy. I don't remember what I said. My mouth was dry. As I shoved him with my arm, the boy fell down, secreted away in shadow behind the rock...

The ocean was deep blue. Harsh heat waves drifted in from it, and I gulped them. I gazed at the sun, which stood still: a sharp, white disk. The boy had fainted in the shadow behind the rock. Casting my eyes back at him as he lay stomach-down on the gray grass, I made my way back along the white streets to my hotel. My mind was numb, but I could clearly recollect that Arab boy's eyes twitching and glittering with pleasure as I tormented him...

I had become a kind of idiot after the trip to Aden. I felt languid. I could muster neither the interest nor the energy to do anything at all. I lay on the bed all day, smoking constantly and casting my cloudy eyes into space. Occasionally there drifted into my mind the livid radiance of the colored rock, and the image of the naked Arab boy face down on his stomach in its dark, emphatic shadow. My mouth twitched and I murmured, "He deserved it." But I couldn't say why he deserved it.

Presently the new school term started. It was the year upperclassmen at Henri IV Secondary School, me included, were to prepare for the test to obtain *le baccalaureat*. The school brought M. Madenier, of the Faculty of Philosophy, University of Lyon, to give a series of philosophy lectures. This old fellow obviously favored wine and meat, which had made his face rosy and round. Hovering above the table his face would appear, and off he went, saying "*Mon petits*" with a sugary smile. I hated that satisfied face. I listened to this Catholic philosopher expatiate upon man's goodness and virtue, or upon the progress of the human mind, or the historical maturity of human civilization, quite as if I were suffering auditory hallucinations. It was ludicrous. My seventeen- and eighteen-year-old classmates, in all their innocence, never doubted the credibility and value of these words, at least at the bottom of their hearts. So why did I find them funny? I didn't, of course, have any logical argument with which to overthrow the old moralist's beliefs. But I knew that I was a cross-eyed boy, I knew about Yvonne and the dog and the wisteria petals in that tableau I had witnessed from the window when I was twelve, I remembered a naked brown girl dancing like a demon on a boy's head in the maze-like streets of Aden, and I could recall the grass burnt by the heat of the sun—that white, burning disk. And then, at the bottom of a rock...Well, that was enough for me.

The next year, my father died. His car crashed into a tree while he was out driving with his mistress. It was the summer of 1938. I didn't wail. I felt no grief. Of course, I no longer believed in God or life eternal.

The test for *le baccalaureat* was given at the Lyon Law College, along the Claude Bernard. On my answer sheet, I wrote out the words M. Madenier had taught us—"the good," "virtue," "the priority of Reason," "historical development," and so on—thinking all the while of the old man's sugary face. When I passed the test, my poor mother cried in happiness, dreaming that, someday, I would become a lawyer. I just smiled in cynicism.

Nothing mattered to me. Anyway, I had probably been deceiving everyone around me ever since the incident with Yvonne and the dog. My father died without knowing the secret of my experience in Aden. My mother hoped I'd open a law office on Republique Street someday. And if everything had remained as it had always been, I might well have continued to conform to the image the adults had of me.

But the following year, the war broke out. Hitler sent his Nazi army into Poland.

# Chapter III

I strolled over to the Law College on the Claude Bernard one hot afternoon in late August, the year before the war. Having passed the test for *le baccalaureat*, I was to matriculate in October.

The college grounds were bright in the severe heat and sun of late summer. There was scarcely anyone about, and it looked like quiet hours at the sanatorium. However, I heard somebody playing the piano clumsily, somewhere off in the distance, perhaps in one of the dormitories.

I found a list of lectures for the upcoming term posted on the bulletin board in the hallway. M. Madenier would teach the *Critique of Pure Reason* by Kant. I recalled the round, rosy face of the good-natured old man. That empty, sodden face epitomized my days at Henri IV Secondary School. On somnolent afternoons, the classroom smelled of jam from lunch, and everybody sat taking notes in silence. *Conscience humane, decision de morale*...Grey ashes were falling over my desk.

I still heard the piano music. It was one of those tunes that I could never remember the title of, even though I had heard it many times. The more corridors I turned into, the further away the music seemed, as if in a dream.

All at once, I heard a girl's voice coming from inside a classroom. I peeped in through the window, standing on my toes.

"No. Give me a clear answer, Marie Thérèse. Are you or are you not going to the dance?" the girl said, sitting on a desk with her feet dangling. She wore a white towel over a bathing suit. It seemed she and her friend were getting ready to swim in the pool in the yard.

"Of course I'd like to go, Monique," answered Marie Thérèse, handing the other girl a bottle of cream, like a maid. "But Jacques...Jacques would never let me. He told me, you know, that it's unseemly for students to be holding dances when Jews are being killed in Germany."

"Jacques? To hell with Jacques. It would be a different story if he were your boyfriend or your fiancé, but he's just a seminarian. He thinks of nothing but theology and missionary work. What does he have to do with your life? You know what? He's always given me the creeps. That grim face of his is full of gloom and fanaticism."

The bathing suit revealed Monique's fleshy, snow-white chest and arms, and her long blonde hair hung down over her shoulders.

"Come on. Listen to me." Monique shook Marie Thérèse by the shoulder. Her head hung down.

"No." Marie Thérèse gave a weak reply. I have to say she was less than beautiful. "I know Jacques is only my cousin, but I lost my parents as a child, and was brought up in his house. I owe him my education."

"You owe him, huh?" Monique sneered, holding a cigarette in her mouth. "Maybe that seminarian loves you."

"No! Loves *me*? But if that's so, why would he enter seminary?"

"Because he's ugly!" Monique laughed shrilly. "He entered seminary because he's ugly and he doesn't have the courage to woo a woman. That's all!"

*Because he's ugly!* These words immediately reminded

me of my cross eyes, and of my father's words when I was a boy: "I'm telling you to look to the right! You won't be popular with the girls. Never."

The two girls left the classroom. I remained there, kneeling. An old movie I once saw popped into my mind for no reason. It was about a hare-lipped man. Because of his deformity, he had never been loved by a woman, and because of his deformity he killed a prostitute who insulted him.

*He was hare-lipped. He was hare-lipped.* I tried to get a grip on the strange voice bursting out inside my head. *He was hare-lipped.*

The girls had tossed their lingerie, light as foam, behind a screen. A sweet scent drifted up from a thin, pink veil. I picked it up. It was so fragile on my fingers that I thought it would melt into my palm. There was a panty hemmed in narrow lace, and a *soutien-gorge* that looked opaque, as if it was finished with wax. It was all so smooth and soft.

*Because he's ugly...Because he's ugly and doesn't have the courage to woo a woman.* With savage force, I tore up the lingerie. A harsh, laughing sound issued from my fingers as the seams ripped, "Eeeeek!" It carried me back to that Arab boy who groaned, and who made that same sound, as the girl trampled him under the burning sun in that maze of Aden...

I heard somebody give a swallow. A man had been watching every move I made, leaning against the wall near the door. The evening sun shone directly on his face through the window, and his glasses glittered. I could see that his forehead was sweaty.

19

He was a very skinny man. His rough cowl made a queer, dry sound when he moved.

*This must be the man the girls were talking about*, I thought.

Somebody started playing the piano again in the dormitory. What was the tune? I'd heard that one, too. Strangely enough, my mind was more focused on remembering the name of the tune than on the man who now stood in front of me.

"*Cochon!*" the man muttered. "Pig! Put it down!"

I gazed at my hands, unconsciously. For the first time, a sense of shame burned my face and head, like boiling water.

"Why? Why should I put it down?"

"I have been watching you," the seminarian said, backpedaling amongst the desks, as if he were shrinking from me. "I saw you."

"So?"

"I know. The filthiest of all the sins of the flesh! I know why you did what you did."

Vacantly I looked at the man's face. His damp forehead betrayed a receding hairline, and some pitiful tufts of red hair remained on top of his head. This man was uglier than ugly cross-eyed me, uglier than that harelip from the movie.

*He entered seminary because he didn't have the courage to woo a woman.*

I felt like laughing. I didn't know why, but I wanted to laugh out loud. "'The filthiest of all the sins of the flesh!' Pshaw!" I threw the lingerie on the floor and stepped into the deserted corridor.

# Chapter IV

On October 2nd, there was an inaugural ceremony at the college. Law students filed into the auditorium wearing, as was traditional, berets with red ribbons. I spotted old Madenier as he sat there proudly, the *Legion d'honneur* displayed on his lecturer's gown. The professors' section was full of solemn faces, serious faces—undernourished, gloomy, bony faces. Students listened as a guest speaker, Jules Romains, the novelist, addressed them.

"War might well break out," said Romains, his voice full of drama. He deliberated a moment, wearing a tragic expression, with his fingers on his forehead. "Valery and I have already sent a resolution to Berlin condemning war. But this resolution, our expression of good will, will likely be trampled into the ground by Nazi boots. I am certain they will reject it. But even so, our ideals will not be vanquished. We must say what we must say."

There was thunderous applause. "That's right!" "*Vive la France!*" shouted the people, deeply impressed. In the late 1930s, France was still pacific. I felt silly.

We had a *bizu* after the ceremony. A *bizu* is a party meant to cultivate friendship between the more senior classes and the freshmen.

Students drank white wine, which had been donated by their parents. There was music, and we played the traditional game of "Electing the King." Law students with red ribbons, literature students with yellow ribbons, female students flushed from drinking—everyone scampered about, laughing. Monique was there with her red scarf, swimming through the crowd.

"Albert is out now!"

"So it is...your turn."

None of the girls asked me, a cross-eyed boy, to join in the games. I guess I should have left the festivities early, but somehow I was savoring this misery, this darkness. I was used to it. From the window, I saw the autumn sun bathe the statue of Auguste Comte out in the quad, turning it golden. A dove flew out in an arc from the dome of the philosophy classroom.

Somebody touched my shoulder. I turned back. The seminarian was standing there, blinking his eyes behind shiny glasses.

"Look," he whispered in his pained, husky voice. "Why don't you come with me?"

"What for?" I asked.

"There is a quiet place over there. Why don't you come with me?"

"But what for?" I repeated.

"I'd like to talk to you."

The seminarian started walking, leading me. We exited the hall and made our way across the quad, where the weakening autumn sun shone to its fullest. I followed in silence behind the cowl, which was sun-bleached a dark brown color.

Sun streamed into the geography classroom between black columns, making striped, flower-like patterns. It was a strangely quiet place, to be sure.

"My name is Jacques," said the seminarian; he cast his eyes down shyly. Sweat gathered over his bald forehead as it had the other day, and the thinning red hair atop his head clumped together like red chili peppers.

"What's this all about?" I asked. I debated whether or not to give my name, and then gave it.

Jacques put his hands into the pockets of his cowl and took out an apple.

"Would you like one?" he asked.

"Oh, the forbidden fruit, huh?" I laughed.

Jacques deflected my remark in his strained voice.

"I'm a seminarian at Fourviere," he said as he bit into the apple and took a seat by one of the poles. "I come here to audit courses. I have to write an essay on canon law. I should have taken time to talk to you the other day. I had no right to accost you."

I noticed for the first time that he used *je* to refer to himself and *tu* to address me.

"No, you didn't," I answered. "You'd been eavesdropping on the conversation between those girls, just as I had."

"I didn't mean to. I was just passing by and..."

"That's enough," I interrupted, and sat down next to him. "I don't trust seminarians. You Catholics lie even to yourselves, you know, and you feel no guilt about it."

"To ourselves?" The seminarian stopped eating his apple and became defiant. "What do you mean?"

"Well, you heard what the girl said, didn't you? She knows why you entered seminary."

Jacques's hands quivered as he held the apple. *The harelip murdered that prostitute in order to lie about his own face. M. Madenier evolved his concepts of "progress" and "improvement" in order to lie about the human face. And Jacques...*

"But I haven't lied to anyone," he said, standing up abruptly and dropping the apple to the ground. "I know I'm

23

ugly. I have been since I was a child. That's why I understood how you, a cross-eyed young man, did the thing you did. I knew I harbored the same jealousy."

*Did I rip up that girl's lingerie out of jealousy? I thought about it hard. No, it couldn't have been mere jealousy, certainly not.*

"It's a curse to be ugly." Jacques was groaning. "It really is. When I was a child, I felt that even my mother and sister averted their eyes from me. But when I grew older, about age fourteen, I understood that my features were like a cross. Jesus bore a cross on his back, and I realized that in my own way I had to bear one, too."

Sweat gathered again on his forehead. Blood vessels swelled out thick and blue on his bald skull, and behind his glasses his eyes grew wet, like those of a rotten fish.

Quite disgusted, I tried to ignore his tear-stained face. But then my father's white swollen hands coalesced in my mind, as if out of the weak autumn light that hung suspended between the columns of the geography classroom.

*To the right. I'm telling you to look to the RIGHT! You won't be popular with the girls. Never.*

Three or four students burst from the hall into the quad, laughing loudly. It appeared that they were scrambling after something. Rossi's sweet song drifted out through the open door.

> *Gather roses while they are young,*
> *Before they shrivel and fade...*

"And so I entered seminary," Jacques murmured, word by word. It seemed he was speaking not to communicate anything to me but somehow to contain himself. "I thought about taking up the cross, and the cross I resolved to bear when I was fourteen has altered. I want to bear the burden not simply of my ugly face but of all the ill-favored faces in the world. Just as Jesus did."

*Go out beneath the blue sky, while the sun is high,*
*And before it darkens with night...*

"The newspapers say more Jews were killed by the Nazis today. Evil pervades Europe. War could erupt at any moment. And, dear God, those students are singing!"

I took the apple gently from the ground, and I bit into it. It was grassy and tart.

"No matter how many crosses you bear," I said, "humanity will be none the better for it. Evil is inexhaustible."

"But if you carry a cross, too," Jacques replied, "if you bear the sorrow at least of being a cross-eyed young man, and if still others take up the cross..." He covered his face with his hands.

"Me?" I said, and cast the sour apple away into the sunlight. It rolled down the quad. "I'll never be intoxicated with my own ugliness, not like you. I won't obsess myself with crosses. Sure, I can be so weak as to tear up a girl's lingerie. But I don't believe in the power of the crucifix."

I went down the quad and stamped on the apple. "Is that all you wanted to talk to me about?"

"I'll pray for you," Jacques murmured, almost spitting his words out, his hands still over his face. "I will. You may not care about God, but God always cares about you."

The students seemed to have all pulled out. I looked back and saw Jacques leaning against the pole, as if he would collapse. His head was pressed against it. He didn't move, and his pose reminded me of Jesus. Like Jesus, he was drunk with himself, determined to take up even a cross-eye's wounds.

25

# Chapter V

He started to attack me. On October 5th, the first day of the new term, I noticed a copy of the *bleu croix* edition of *Imitation of Christ* on my desk. And that wasn't all. On the back of the cover, my name was written, and not in a neat hand, together with a phrase from *The Gospel According to John.*

I considered going to school early the next morning to return the book to him, but I didn't. There was no particular reason to do it.

This childish game persisted. Like clockwork, *Saint Theresa* by Dognac, or *Spiritual Exercises* by St. Ignatius Loyola, would arrive, week after week.

I didn't so much as crack the books, and was never much bothered by the silly charade. Still, I couldn't ignore that seminarian. The attempts of a naive seminarian to seduce me were nothing, but all the same, he had witnessed my secret in that empty classroom two months ago. His voice had pierced my body like a gimlet as he blurted out, "The filthiest of all the sins of the flesh!"

"You are cross-eyed. I understand the pain of being cross-eyed." Nothing hurt me more than pity from this "amen" lot.

I decided to await an opportunity in silence.

It was the end of June of the next year when I had, through sheer luck, the chance to take my revenge. It happened in the Law College Library after class. I had been sitting for two hours in front of a law book packed with black, tiny characters. The sun was setting. The windows were already dim and gray. We were entering upon the season when the yellowish mists of Lyon would creep up from its two rivers, the Saone and the Rhone. My mind wandered from thought to thought. I closed the law book and took from my bag *The Joy of Faith*, or something like it, which Jacques had left for me that day.

Jacques had underlined and circled passages in red here and there. I read the book out of curiosity, but nothing worthwhile occurred to me. I got bored and was about to close the book when I realized I had overlooked something important.

It was a note, a kind of afterthought, which Jacques had written in the margin of the last page. "Can he mean that Christ never agonized? He had been inflicted with mental anguish twice." Jacques used the passive voice: *had been inflicted*. "One time was in the Garden of Gethsemane when He anticipated his persecution and torture the following day. He sweated blood. The other time was when Judas betrayed Him. For who can say Jesus didn't love Judas?"

*Judas*...I racked my brains. The church steeple floated in blackish blue beyond the window. I saw a flock of doves fly across the indigo sky. Why hadn't I noticed it before? Why hadn't I seen that the surest way to torment a Christian is to read the Bible backward, so to speak? But then, *who* is Jacques's Judas?

I was about to leave the library when I realized I had left my umbrella in the classroom. I went back along the hallway, which was as deserted as it had been that first afternoon in August. And oddly enough, I heard a voice, again, issuing from the classroom. Everything was exactly as it had been on that first day. I sensed that something was going on, and that Jacques was there. I peeped in through a window between the corridor and the room. Jacques stood with his back to me, Monique opposite him.

At first, I couldn't make out what it was they were disputing.

Marie Thérèse was crying. She wore her nut-brown hair in pigtails, like a fourteen- or fifteen-year-old girl, and it hung over her shoulders. A white blouse and gray skirt wrapped her scrawny body. Her body was still stiff and "green" and mean compared with Monique's, whose white breasts and hips were ripe.

"Marie Thérèse!" Jacques shouted. The body of the girl twitched as if she had been beaten. "You heard the bishop at church last week, didn't you? I mean the part where he said we Christians must sacrifice, today more than ever. I know you heard him say we must see to our behavior, that we must do it for the people suffering in Germany, and to prevent the outbreak of war."

Monique took over, raising her eyebrows. "But what's wrong with a little dance?" Then she turned to the girl. "Marie Thérèse, why are you afraid of this seminarian? You needn't be."

It was just as Monique had said. Each time Jacques shouted, Marie Thérèse turned her head aside like a puppy, and, step-by-step, crept farther back behind her friend.

"I'm not talking to you," bellowed the seminarian to Monique, by now quite upset. "I have nothing to do with you. But I am responsible for Marie Thérèse. She didn't enter college to attend dances."

"Well, what did she enter for, then? Tell me."

Jacques was silent for some time. I could see his bald forehead shine with sweat, just as it had that day.

"What did she come here for?" Monique pressed him.

28

"Let Marie Thérèse answer that," replied Jacques. "I won't."

The girl collapsed into a chair, her face in her hands. The three fell silent, motionless.

"I won't go," the girl said through her sobs. "I won't go. Don't worry about me, Monique."

"Well, is that it?" Monique muttered, her spirit damped. She stared at Marie Thérèse with a look of scorn. "Bye-bye."

I slipped into the next classroom to hide myself. A door slammed loudly, and then I heard Monique running along the corridor.

The classroom had grown gray. In the dusk, Jacques and the girl looked like stone statues. It was hushed.

"Marie Thérèse," the seminarian whispered, his hands on her shoulders. "You can go if you want to." His voice was surprisingly tender. "I hope you don't think that I prevent you from going. All I wanted was that your..."

"It is all for the sake of my soul, isn't it?" Marie Thérèse said. She stood up abruptly and looked at the seminarian with hateful eyes. "For the sake of my soul, my faith, and my duty."

"Marie Thérèse..."

A faint smile crossed my lips. At that moment I understood who Jacques's Judas would be.

The next day, I hid behind the plane trees along the Rhone in front of the gate out of which all the students surge, and waited for Marie Thérèse. It was hot. The students emerged, melancholy and languid after the day's labors. Soon, the seminarian appeared in his black cowl, his arms crossed, leading Marie Thérèse. As always, his bald forehead and glasses glittered.

The two walked toward the Guillotière Bridge. I followed them, hiding behind the trees every now and then.

They entered St. Bernard's Church at the foot of the bridge. I waited for some ten minutes, leaning against a wall stained with doves' droppings.

The girl came out by herself, holding a red bag. She headed to the bus stop on Republique Street.

The bus arrived and I jumped on before it moved off.

"Marie Thérèse," I said to her. She looked back. Her face, with its spattering of freckles, blushed. "Is this your route?"

"Yes," she replied, in a voice so small and weak that I could hardly hear her. She hung onto the strap and fixed her eyes outside the window. She must never have been addressed by a man.

"Are you going to the dance, the day after tomorrow?"

She cast her face down, embarrassed and anxious. "Um..."

"No? Why not?" I asked.

Marie Thérèse bit her lips.

"How come?" I asked again.

"Well..."

The bus turned between the City Hall and the Opera. Marie Thérèse lost her balance and leaned into me. I felt her skinny, bony body.

"You know," I said, "the other day, I asked Jacques for his permission because I want you to dance with me."

My sweaty hand touched hers. Marie Thérèse hastily pulled it away.

"And we ended up arguing. Over you," I said, as I pulled my body closer to hers. "I told him his Catholicism was too narrow, too strict. True Catholicism isn't like that. It's more tolerant, bigger. Don't you agree?"

My first goal was to flatter the ugly girl's vanity. I told her I wouldn't go to the dance unless she did.

"Look. You're not to blame."

"But..." Her face was completely red, even her ears. "But it doesn't have to be *me*. There are a lot of girls."

A carnival had set up along the Cours Lafayette. The roadside was lined with pavilions and bustled with the people. It was boring, all so boring.

"Who," I replied disconsolately, "who on earth is going to dance with a cross-eyed man?"

"Oh, no!" Suddenly Marie Thérèse looked at me with sad eyes full of pity.

"Well...Will *you*?"

"But if Jacques learns..."

The bus stopped in front of a plaza. Marie Thérèse was to get off here.

"You will come, won't you?" Again and again I whispered into her ear.

I gloated as Marie Thérèse's stiff body disappeared into the crowd of children and mothers making their way home from the carnival. Anyway, the girl now had a small secret to keep from Jacques, and I knew that small secrets bear lies, and that lies bear still more secrets, and eventually tumble down into the valley of betrayal...

# Chapter VI

On the night of the dance, I met Marie Thérèse at the bottom of the bronze statue of Louis XIV in the Bellecour Plaza. She looked ludicrous. Her face was dappled with powder, and she even had rouge on her lips. Not even Jacques could have forborne turning away from this clownish face. She had gone to the trouble of hauling out a black velvet cape to wear. She gave a coquettish smile when she saw me. I was amazed at how deftly a simple betrayal and one secret had transformed this girl into a woman.

*At this very moment, Jacques would be burying his face in* Summa Theologica *or something in his dormitory room at Fourviere seminary.*

Already I could hear the sweet tango music and jovial voices drifting out from the hall at the Hotel l'Amour. Someone was tuning up a saxophone. Light streamed out of the windows, shimmering like a spring night. The students at the reception desk stifled giggles, pulling each other's sleeves, as I escorted Marie Thérèse into the lobby.

"I wonder if Monique is already here," she said.

"Don't worry about her. She'll be more surprised if you turn up later anyway," I said, affecting the blunt tone of a boyfriend.

A lone bartender manned the bar, drying glasses.

"Cognac."

"No, I can't drink," the girl said as she took off her cape, exposing her obtrusive and unsightly collarbones. Her

32

chest was completely flat, like that of a seven- or eight-year-old girl.

"Just try a sip. It's nothing, you know. By the way, you didn't tell Jacques, did you?"

"I trusted you," replied Marie Thérèse, distorting her face painfully.

"Everything will be all right. Don't worry."

As she got drunk, Marie Thérèse's face gradually flushed. Sweat started to wash her makeup away, revealing her freckles. Even her neck began to wobble, like that of a broken doll.

"I trust you," she repeated, tongue-tied.

I waited for the waltz music to start in the hall upstairs. I had a reason for choosing a waltz rather than a tango or a slow dance.

When the Jacques Brothers Band started to play a new tune called "Casually," I thought the time was right. I pushed Marie Thérèse into the crowd of girls who looked like spinning tops in red, yellow, and blue.

"I trust you," the foolish girl babbled out. "I trust you."

I turned often to prevent her from catching her breath.

Marie Thérèse pressed her face against my chest. I worried that what was left of her sweaty makeup would ruin my "Sunday best."

"Oh, I can't go on. I can't breathe," Marie Thérèse said, wilting in my arms. She panted for breath, her mouth open like a dog's, exposing her pink tongue. "I want some water."

At the left end of the hall was a passage leading to the garden. Nobody was out there yet. I seated her on a bench behind a bush.

I could see the electric news bulletin in the Bellecour Plaza clearly from where we sat. I fetched some water from the bar, with a considerable amount of gin in it. Marie Thérèse drank it down in one draught to slake her thirst. I lifted her face with my right hand, holding her arms tightly with my left.

"Not one single man has ever paid attention to me," she said, clinging to my body. "Nobody has loved me."

The electric news bulletins flashed on and off. *The Nazis...Slaughtered...Fifty Jews...In Kern.* A jitterbug and the drawling sound of a trumpet emerged from the hall. Firecrackers followed. *The Nazis...Slaughtered...Fifty Jews...In Kern.* "Yeah. Right," I murmured absently.

The night breeze woke me up. The girl lay sprawled on the bench, like a corpse. That Arabian boy had lain like that behind the brown rock in the bright sun of Aden. Something like desolation tugged at my heart, though I don't know why. And it would be more accurate to say that it was fatigue, a deep fatigue, rather than sorrow. Once I had had my fill, I didn't know what to do next. The ball-like sun in the leaden sky above Aden had a dull, shining corolla, and my soul was like that now, burning in blue.

I went back out to the lobby alone. I saw the seminarian standing amongst the chairs, staring at me, but what did I care?

"Where is she?" Jacques shook me by the shoulders. "Where is Marie Thérèse?"

"Out in the garden, I guess," I replied, exhausted. I felt intense power in his fingers.

"You...Don't tell me that you..."

"Oh, stop it. I didn't so much as lay a finger on her. Why do you carry on like that? Is it because I once tore up

her lingerie? You've torn up something much more important to her than that."

"Why do you…" Jacques started to speak, but cut
himself short. He shuddered like a man with a fever.
"Devil!" he shouted, raising his fist. But soon enough his
hand dropped away weakly.

I didn't see them after that. Summer vacation began the
following day.

# Chapter VII

During the vacation, my mother took me with her to Combloux, a resort in Savoy to which she retreated for her health. She was almost neurotic with the fear of having a stroke. But I don't know if the light air of the highland—it was nearly a thousand meters above sea level—was quite good for her blood pressure. We checked into two rooms at a small hotel on the outskirts of the village. I spent my time reading books about Jansenism. I wanted to think through a few ideas that had formed me, in some way or another, since childhood. I was interested in Jansenism for only one reason: The doctrine held that we human beings are indelibly stained by original sin. No matter how hard we struggle, we always descend into the abyss of evil. No virtue, no will, can ever be strong enough to purify us. These ideas sorted well with my view of humanity.

Knowing nothing at all about this, my mother was satisfied to see me reading religious books again after my long negligence. Poor, naive mother! She had no idea what fruit had been borne of the strict religious education she gave her little boy in that house in the Croix Rousse.

It was quiet, day in and day out. The summer was so deep and dense as to dye all the highlands in blue. I bought two postcards and wrote "*Bonne Vacance*" on each of them. One I sent to Jacques, and the other to Marie Thérèse. I got no reply, of course. September came. Mist filled the air; it was growing cooler. Now my mother started to worry about asthma. Packing up for the return to Lyon early on the morning of September 1st, I learned that the German army had invaded Poland...

I hurried to the college on October 1st, just as soon as the vacation ended. Everything was quiet. The schedule of lectures for the new term fluttered on the campus billboard. The scene looked just as it had in peacetime. A tableau of shorthaired female students were copying down the schedule, their heads inclined.

Plato—Lecturer, Madenier

When I saw the name, I remembered vividly the old teacher's round face: rose-colored and flushed from wine, a sugary smile always on his lips, and a beard yellow with cigarette tar. He had taught Introductory Ethics to my class, his face bent down toward the desk, when I was a student at Henri IV. And even now, with war and wholesale slaughter pending, the old man would interpret Plato, wearing a dissembling smile. M. Madenier would live; his life was granted. And not only that, his good-natured smile would govern a university classroom. That was all possible, even now.

I left the College of Humanities and walked across the lawn. When I reached the statue of Auguste Comte, I spotted Marie Thérèse at the gate, holding a red bag and whispering something to Monique.

"Bonjour, Monique." I made sure to greet the friend first. Then I swallowed and came to a halt. "Bonjour, Marie Thérèse," I said, staring into her eyes.

Marie Thérèse didn't offer her hand. Instead, she inched herself back, like a shy little girl, until she hid behind Monique.

"What did you do afterward?—I mean, the night of the dance. Did you stay at the hotel?" I spoke with deliberate familiarity. "What's the matter with you?"

Marie Thérèse blurted something out so sharply as to cause Monique to look back out of reflex. I couldn't catch what she said. But it didn't matter to me.

"I guess we'll never have another dance. You know, we'll be at war soon," I said, addressing only Monique, with a smile. I left the place.

My mother had her stroke. The mental shock of her native country waging war against her husband's country might have been part of the cause. I say this because she shouted, in her delirium, "I'm not German! I'm French!" She must have been seeing her husband in a dream. Her voice had about it a certain voluptuousness, a certain coquettishness. It was as if she were trying to affirm her love and rectitude to her dead husband. Sometimes I felt pity for the woman, as I sat beside her.

I used her illness as an excuse to take a leave of absence from school. She would never have permitted such a thing when she was healthy. But she interpreted it as a natural expression of filial duty on my part, in keeping with the popular illusion.

And illusion still enveloped Lyon. Conquering Poland in a trice, the Nazis were poised to invade France. The newspapers wrote, "Look at them. They can't make a move because they are intimidated by our Maginot line." The citizens of Lyon sat on the terraces of cafes in the autumn sun, with golden marronnier leaves falling, drinking their aperitifs for hours on end, the younger ones yawning, the older ones mulling over old memories of World War I.

Autumn was drawing to a close. We were entering the season when the yellowish mists particular to Lyon crept up from the rivers the Saone and the Rhone, licking their way through the city. My mother took a turn for the worse. "Sonny, you must go to church," she muttered, looking at me vacantly from the bed. Lately, she confused me with the little boy I used to be fifteen years ago—a boy as pure and pious as an angel. "This is it. She's dying," I thought. After the nurse went home, I applied medicine to her pus-ridden back to relieve her bedsores, thinking of the "freedom" I would regain on the day she died. It reminded me of the freedom I enjoyed in Aden when my father left for Port Said. Still, gazing into my mother's earth-colored face, which was drenched with sweat, I wasn't happy. I had turned to stone.

In a spell of misty, cold rain in February 1940, my mother died. She knew no more about her son's dark secrets than his father had when he met his end. She breathed her last breath with her angel-boy holding her hands.

Now I was alone. My inheritance would secure me for the next ten years. I was free.

Another arousing spring came on. From the windows upstairs, I looked down on the street with its wisteria blossoms falling. It was deserted, as it had been on that other day. Light purple petals fell in the hush. The old dog died long ago, of course. And I'd heard nothing of the maid Yvonne.

I didn't know what had become of Jacques and Marie Thérèse, either. I didn't care about them anymore. I went to

39

the university a few times, but my old classmates were quickly forgetting about me.

So I wasn't particularly surprised when I heard about Marie Thérèse from Monique.

"Heavens! Didn't you know?" said Monique. "Marie Thérèse is boarding at the convent of St. Bernadette."

"Was it Jacques' idea?" I asked.

"I should think so!" said this modern girl. Then she added, with a sarcastic smile, "Go to St. Bernard's at five. The couple will be praying together."

A week or so later, I decided to visit the church after all. It was a languid evening. I remembered following Marie Thérèse there sometime last June, a year ago. But I hadn't visited it since.

A big magnolia tree grew by the church, its white flowers in bloom. The flowers stood out as if floating, white in the gray evening haze. I went into the chancel. But they hadn't turned up yet. I took a seat by the worn-out prayer stools and waited.

Altar candles burned with their red flames, illuminating the crucifix that stood on the altar. Jesus—ugly, bony, and naked—hung on the cross, his hands and feet nailed down, his head drooping toward me. On the base was engraved a Latin phrase, "I Give You Life." A figure of the Virgin Mary knelt by the base, collapsed in grief, clasping her hands together.

I had seen many crucifixes like this. Though I was brought up Protestant, I knew a little about Catholic art. It wasn't hard to see that the crucifix at St. Bernard's had little value as art; on the contrary, it was done in the popular style. Nevertheless, this image of Christ profoundly tempted me, who had come merely to steal a glimpse of Jacques and Marie Thérèse.

What I realized was this: Jesus' life had its consummation in torture. "Christ" he may have been, but he could never get round a world that consists of the torturers and the tortured. Hundreds of millions of followers pass through church gates every Sunday, coins jingling in their pockets. They kneel in front of crucifixes. They hear vacantly what the ministers and priests preach, but they never listen to what that crucifix is telling them, right in front of their eyes. They never really see that the life that carpenter's son led unfolded, after all, in the very world that the maid and the old dog dwelt in along the Croix Rousse, the very world I inhabited when I pushed that boy down in the shadow of the rock.

*Yes, isn't that right?* Christ whispered to me. But I shook my head. It was as if he meant to seduce me, preying on my most vulnerable points. I groaned: *None of your tricks, now!*

When I came to myself and looked around, Marie Thérèse and Jacques were already here, placing votive candles on the prickets in front of the Virgin Mary.

The girl was thinner now. She wore a loose black garment, the sort an old maid teacher at a girls' school might wear, together with a pair of black socks. She clenched her teeth and pressed her fists to her face, while Jacques just stood next to her, crossing his arms and closing his eyes, just as he had done long ago. His pathetic red hair glistened with sweat along his receding hairline. The candle flames reflected off his rimless glasses as he made his small movements. With him, all was the same as before.

I had no idea why it was that Marie Thérèse alone had changed. I imagine, though, that she must have been severely admonished by Jacques since the night of that dance. She must have been driven into a corner. He must have demanded that she repent, that she redeem herself from the sins of the flesh she committed with me. But what I certainly knew, and what was of great significance to me at this moment, was that the girl was utterly under the tyrannical control of Jacques. The girl I ruined—and precisely because I ruined her—must readily have fallen prey to the fanatical seminarian. She was back in Jacques's hands.

I pressed my cheek to a fat, cold, stone pillar in the chancel, feeling inexpressible rage and shame. It wasn't so much against them that I felt it as against myself, who was living, alone, in the world of M. Madenier and Jacques...

The Nazis broke through the border at Holland and Belgium on May 10th. The mythic Maginot line collapsed!

Railway stations in Lyon were in chaos, with refugees pouring in from Northern France and Paris, together with newly mustered officers and soldiers and their families. In expectation of air raids, we were forbidden to go out after five o'clock.

On June 25th, Paris finally fell. And within a week, the people of Lyon woke, flustered, to the sounds of the orderly footsteps of the Nazi soldiers, and to the vibrations of the Nazi tanks, drifting in through the morning mists of the Rhone.

The occupation had begun. The doors of all the stores and houses were tightly shut. Cafes and movie theaters remained closed till four o'clock. People were scared to go out in the streets. Plane trees lined Republique Street, their wilted leaves dangling in the intense heat of July. Only the Nazis' motorbikes and sidecars sped along, making their sharp, ripping sound.

I shut myself up inside the house. I waited. I simply waited for something to happen.

The day of execution, torture, and slaughter was coming. The day was coming when humanity would tear off its mask of "civilization" and "progress" and show its true countenance. Yvonne and the old dog, the Arabian girl and her boy in Aden, the burnt, brown grassland and that rock under a still, white sun. Soon, *that* world would return to its true self. I knew it.

I was out in the city on some business, in the bright August sunshine. The people, somewhat used to the occupation by now, were walking about, relieved.

And then it happened. Out of the blue, I heard the roar of German sidecars, with trucks rolling in behind. Instinctively I hid myself behind the closed door of a store.

I heard the shrill scream of a woman. Armed Nazi soldiers leapt out of the trucks and dove into the crowd of people, who now scattered in all directions, panicked. They seized several men, at random, beating them as they dragged them along, eventually stuffing them into the truck. All this happened in a minute. And then the trucks sped away.

We couldn't discern their purpose. Obviously, the men had been singled out by chance. "I wonder if they were from the Resistance," whispered the people as they gathered in little groups here and there along the streets. French Vichy policemen arrived shortly and directed us to go home at once. The people dispersed, casting their eyes back, again and again.

The next day, we learned the reason for the raid. Pictures of the distorted faces of the five arrestees were pasted all over the city.

"The Army of Occupation, Lyon, has decided to execute these five Frenchmen in retaliation for the murder, by the Resistance, of the loyal German Sgt. Hans Mueller. Let it be known that, from now on, we will demand five French lives for every German soldier killed."

I was thoroughly impressed by the deliberation that lay behind the Nazi terrorism. Their techniques could be described only as scientific, so efficient were they at withering the French with horror and fear.

Down through the nineteenth century, the reign of terror and torture had been essentially rather impulsive, animalistic. Men starved for blood, or crazed with rage and fear, were simply swept up into all the torturing and the killing, by impulse. This primitive sort of urge lay behind the Inquisition and the French Revolution.

The Nazis, however, were modern, thoroughly "twentieth century." They knew, with a cold logic, how to make men vulnerable and enslave them. We use the same terms for it: torture and slaughter. But the Nazis had the callous strength of a scientist killing his guinea pigs.

For example, the Nazis refused to give salt to the prisoners in the Polish camps. Sodium is essential for people fatigued by excessive labor. Without it, the prisoners would weaken, day by day, and eventually die from exhaustion. Officially, death from exhaustion isn't "murder." So the Nazis could attribute it all to "natural causes" under the terms of International Law. What's more, this is a very efficient way to kill off large numbers of people quickly.

The roundup I witnessed was most deliberate. Those innocent men became victims simply because they happened to be in town that day, simply because they chanced to be in the wrong place at the wrong time. The idea that a mere whim might bring on death spreads terror better than anything else. If there were only some law, or some rule, that determined who was to die, we could protect ourselves by adhering to it, but there was nothing we could do to thwart chance. After the incident, the people of Lyon could no longer leave their houses. Going out just might mean death.

The Resistance was gradually getting bolder around that time. But each time the Nazis held an execution, the names of the dead members of the Maquis were posted along the main streets. I was surprised to see that being a Jew was a kind of prerequisite for execution. "Pierre Bahn is to be executed for being a Jew." The French knew the Germans hated Jews, and whenever they saw the postings, they were secretly relieved not to have any Jewish blood in their veins. And at that moment, in fact, they inwardly betrayed and abandoned Pierre Bahn, the man who'd been killed. They forgot that Bahn was their fellow Frenchman in addition to being a Jew. The Nazis schemed to divide the French, availing themselves of the meaner instincts of self-preservation.

Once I understood the plot, I looked forward to my trips downtown each evening. The setting sun dyed the wide streets, where nothing was stirring. The whole place was dead, as if it had been ruined for centuries. Looking at the lifeless city, I sometimes wondered how M. Madenier was making out, and what Jacques and the girl were doing. The deserted asphalt street was painted red, as with blood, by the evening light, and it reminded me of the wilderness, or the desert. The scene moved me. I believed I saw truth in it.

One day in early October, I saw an advertisement for a job in the *Progress*, which had gone under Nazi control. The German army needed an interpreter and clerk. But the listing differed from the usual ones: It had been placed by the Gestapo unit attached to the Army of Occupation in Lyon.

Since my mother had been German, I could speak the language to some extent. I stared at the advertisement for

more than an hour, drinking the bitter, sugarless coffee sub-
stitute. I knew what the job would bring to me. Abruptly, my
mother's deathbed words came to mind and bitterness per-
vaded me: "I'm not a German!" she'd shouted in delirium. "I
am French!" *Don't do it. Are you going to betray us? Don't
do it!* I could almost hear her imploring me, desperate.

All the same, I made my way to a black, cold building
behind the Lyon City Court along the Saone. A German soldier with a gun demanded that I show my ID. I told him I
had seen the advertisement in the morning papers. I was led
into a small room that smelled of urine. I saw a man with a
moustache and drawn cheeks waiting there, dispirited. He
said he was Spanish. His right ear was missing.

"I lost it during the Revolution," the man said, in
French. We sat face to face in the evening sun, in silence.

In due time, it was my turn to be called in. In a cold
room with bare walls, a fat, middle-aged lieutenant sat at
his desk. His flabby, sagging skin caught my eyes. It was
hard to believe that this man worked for the Gestapo. After
each question about my career, he blinked listlessly. His eyes
were cloudy and wet, like those of a rotten fish washed up
on the shore. *Is he an alcoholic?* I thought. His eyes
reminded me of my father's.

The afternoon sun gradually receded from the window.
The lieutenant switched on a desk lamp and continued to
take down my answers on the document.

All of a sudden, I heard a scream in the distance, which
sounded like the groan of a wild beast. The scream subsided
for a moment, then rose, again, in a sharp cry. And then all
was hushed. The lieutenant didn't so much as raise his eyes.
I got the job.

# Chapter VIII

Pomme de Pin is the name of a long slope that falls right at the boundary of the Fourviere Hills and the Croix Rousse. I think it reasonable that the Gestapo should have chosen it as the site for their interrogations. The downtown district is conspicuous, and other neighborhoods are thick with apartments and houses. But at Pomme de Pin an extensive earthen wall completely shields the house. Here, the howls, the screams, and other evidence of torture would never reach the outside, with the wide expanse of the yards intercepting it all.

A powerful Lyon landholder owned the manor house at Pomme de Pin before the occupation. And manor though it was, it nevertheless had the look of a large farmhouse. Two cottages had been built in the yard for the tenant farmers, which were connected to the kitchen of the main house by underpasses. It was the kitchen that the Gestapo chose for their interrogations. I know little about the other rooms of the house. I wasn't allowed to roam without an escort.

They took me out to the house for the first time in January 1941. The lieutenant strapped me into a sidecar and drove from Gestapo headquarters out behind the Rhone Court to the lonely estate of Pomme de Pin.

It was twilight. The yellowish mist of Lyon tangled itself up as it crept and licked over the snow, which remained from a fall a few days before. The frozen snow gleamed bluish black, standing out in the dusk. I followed the lieutenant in silence, listening as his boots crunched in the snow. He gave no hint as to why I had been brought here, or as to what I was expected to do.

The windows of the manor house were tightly closed with shutters whose paint was peeling off. Everything was hushed, save for the occasional sound of a branch crackling out in the coppice, which was withered with winter. A few thorny shrubs had crept up over a wall, which was the color of sea cucumbers. I reckoned they were roses. An image of wisteria flowers, falling on a sunlit street in the Croix Rousse, somehow popped into my mind, and soon disappeared.

We entered from the front of the kitchen. A German soldier in an overcoat was leaning against the door, holding a rifle in his arms. He was young. Giving a salute, he inserted a large key into the lock and let the lieutenant and me in.

The kitchen was unlit. Two men sat on shabby wooden chairs in the darkness. They stood up when they recognized us. I looked around as the lieutenant spoke to the men in whispers. A big frying pan hung from the wall, part of which had been stained by decades of smoke and soot from the stove. Three German mess kits sat by the sink.

The lieutenant gestured me over and introduced me to the men. They weren't Germans. In the gray dusk, I made out a long, bony face drenched in sweat; its eyes gave off a queer, feverish glitter.

"I have a consumption," the man said in German, with an accent, while holding his hands in his pockets. He was a Czechoslovakian by the name of Alexandre Ludwig.

The other man, one Andre Chavanne, simply kept staring at me like an idiot. He had an extraordinarily white face, almost translucent. I offered him my hand, but instead of taking it he just kept looking at me with his bloodshot eyes. "Why don't you say howdy-do?" asked Alexandre in his husky voice, chuckling. "You're both French." He coughed dryly and spit on the floor. But Andre Chavanne moved back to the end of the room and leaned against the wall, motionless.

Interrogations were conducted in the kitchen, as was the torture.

With a little experience, I was able to tell whether or not a suspect would be able to endure the torture just by looking at him, as he was dragged up from the small cellar next to the kitchen. I saw a farmer who had sheltered members of the Maquis, a young banker who had relayed notes for the Resistance, a printer who had confidentially printed anti-Nazi propaganda, and so on. They screamed and fainted dead away. But when they clenched their teeth, when they groaned in unbearable pain, often their faces looked quite beautiful.

However, I was little better than a machine for translating the lieutenant's words into French, as he courteously and listlessly questioned his suspects.

"Why don't you tell me the name of the man from the Maquis whom you sheltered?"

"I don't know it. I just gave him medicine and food."

"Why did he choose your house, then?"

"Somebody knocked on the door in the middle of the night on the twelfth. My sister opened the door and found a man from the Maquis, wounded. But after we gave him food and medicine he left, quickly."

"All right then. I had hoped you might spare us this trouble." The lieutenant uttered even these final words languidly.

And then, with a slow movement, Alexandre removed his jacket. The suspect still hardly believed he was to be tortured. He looked appraisingly at the lieutenant's sleepy face, anxious. A blow from a thick hose knocked him out of his chair. Then would fall the dull, but heavy lashes, delivered metronomically. Some suspects would endure the pain in silence for a while, but once they let out a groan, the cries would grow increasingly louder and rise in pitch, like a drunkard's nasal whine. The victim would cry out ever higher, as if to the dry rhythm of the lashes. He would cover his face with his arms. He would squirm across the floor like a green caterpillar, still with his arms over his face. Alexandre's countenance was drenched with sweat, and his eyes glittered with a truly bewitching pleasure. Even the tortured man's voice seemed to me to imply that he now took sensual pleasure in being beaten. As the groans became black roars, Alexandre lashed and lashed, taking his breaths in gasps. "Ugnh, ugnh, ugnh!" he would shout, occasionally spitting out dark phlegm. The lieutenant gave the scene an abstracted gaze, from a corner of the dim kitchen. "Looks like I myself might die before long!" the torturer with the diseased lung would murmur, as if in delirium, spittle staining his lips.

After a while, Alexandre would exhaust himself to the point where he could hardly speak. And when he stopped the beating, his eyes went hollow and black, as they might when the pleasure of lust suddenly ebbed.

Then Andre Chavanne would rise. He would bring a tin of water from the sink and pour it over the prostrate victim's head.

I learned that the character of a tortured man's cries and moans varied with the personality of the torturer. When Alexandre beat them, I detected something more than torture, something like the play of a lascivious desire. This tubercular man derived an intoxicated sort of pleasure from beating, from physically tormenting, another person. And I wondered if his benumbing pleasure infected the victim, for I fancied I could hear something of that in the groans and screams.

But I sensed none of this when Andre Chavanne did the beatings. All I could hear were the dull, hard sounds of his hose sinking into the flesh. Somehow I was interested in this man who simply did his job in silence, his pale face cast down, his nut-brown hair over his forehead, never once shouting or swearing at the victim as Alexandre did. Maybe it was because he really wasn't intoxicated by it all. He had been born French, and had betrayed his country. Yet he was unable to become quite German, no matter what. The gloom of the outcast hung over his pale, bony face. As I listened to him beat the men, I often thought he was beating himself as well. Not others alone would curse him; he also cursed himself. And it certainly distorted him.

As I came to know these men, however, I saw that the torturer isn't simply a savage, violent man, as is generally believed. One evening, I found the lieutenant playing the piano that had been abandoned in the manor house. His cloudy eyes, eyes like those of a rotten fish, now shone with life. The setting sun gave a rosy tint to his forehead, and to his silver hair.

"Do you like music?" I asked.

"Me?" the lieutenant asked, his face instantly contorted. "I like Mozart. Before I was drafted, we used to play Mozart every night together, my wife and children and I. Mozart is sublime."

51

When we didn't have any interrogations to conduct out at Pomme de Pin, I typed and organized cards in the lieutenant's office.

The lieutenant didn't entirely trust me yet. I was forbidden from straying out of the office alone. Still, classifying the cards and making carbons, I was impressed at how efficient and meticulous the Gestapo had been. The cards held nothing more than background information about the French merchants who provisioned the Army of Occupation, or about the refugees who settled in Lyon. Nevertheless, the data comprised not merely their careers, their facial features, their peculiarities, but every little detail about their personal lives— their favorite restaurants, the names of people with whom they associated, their relatives' occupations, and sometimes even the names of lovers and mistresses. "Maybe they know everything about me, too," I thought. How could I say they hadn't entered my house while I was out? After my mother died, I hired a maid named Lacene to come in three times a week. She might well have been a tool of the Nazis, or for that matter of the Resistance. I was living in a time when you had to treat mere passers-by with suspicion. But no matter how closely the lieutenant, or the Gestapo, or the Resistance scrutinized my life, they could never uncover my real past, what really nurtured me: the scene of Yvonne and the old dog, the incident with the boy in Aden. There, I had beheld things that even the lieutenant and Alexandre and Chavanne could never deprive me of; and that marked the fundamental difference between them and me.

In this way, January and February of 1941 passed. We hadn't been out to Pomme de Pin for some time when the lieutenant stepped into the office one day, while I was busy typing. He looked exhausted, as he usually did. Immediately I sensed we were going to do an interrogation. He always looked languid before the interrogations.

"You attended the University of Lyon in 1938, didn't you?" the lieutenant asked me.

I remained silent, my fingers resting on the typewriter keys. I had a feeling that they'd found out something about me, or that their suspicions had in some way been aroused.

"Do you know this man?" the lieutenant asked.

He tossed a photograph on my desk. It was of a young man, but it was yellowed and blurry, perhaps owing to a clumsy job of printing and washing. The man in the photo stared out at me with his small, dark eyes, wide open behind a pair of rimless glasses, and with his head aslant. He looked scared.

"Oh!" I gave a little cry.

"You recognize him?"

"Yes, I do. He is a seminarian."

"Is his name Jacques Monge?"

"Yes, it is."

"That's what I thought."

"What did he do to get arrested?" I asked.

"What did this guy do? He was a liaison for the Maquis in the sixth arrondissement. How wily those Catholic priests are! They can read Mass, all the while engaging in insurrection."

"So you'll conduct an interrogation?"

That afternoon, the lieutenant seated me with him in the sidecar. Everything was the same. The yellow mists of Lyon had already enveloped the estate at Pomme de Pin. No Frenchmen were in sight along the quiet slope. *Jacques, you...are...,* I was about to say to myself, *you...are...a member of the Maquis!* But I quashed the thought. *No, actually this is precisely what I might have expected of you. Of course you would do it.* I recollected the young man's sweaty face, as he shouted in that classroom, as sun streamed in through the windows: "The filthiest of all the sins of the flesh!" A summer afternoon, three years ago now.

The lieutenant stepped out of the sidecar and walked quietly in the dreary wind; his leather boots squeaked in the snow. The shutters were tightly locked over the windows, the better to prevent any cries from slipping out. Again I heard cold, sharp cracking sounds drifting in from the coppice in its winter decay.

As usual, a soldier waited at the door to the kitchen. He wore a steel helmet and a thick overcoat, with a rifle hanging from his shoulder by a strap. Alexandre was pacing around the kitchen, coughing; Jacques was leaning against a wall in the corner.

"Have you done it?" the lieutenant asked.

Alexandre shrugged his shoulders.

The windowpanes rattled. I closed my eyes and thought of the gray wind scouring the yard. It seemed to me that the wind had blown like this for thousands of years, and would for thousands more—rattling, all the while, the windowpanes. The kitchen itself would someday fall to ashes. But the attitude I took as I tortured would remain behind, like the gray wind. The lieutenant, Alexandre, and Chavanne would all die, but another lieutenant and another Alexandre and another Chavanne would appear to take their places. Jacques believed that someday we would overcome this intractable orientation of mankind. But I didn't. Men like this were immortal, and I held them in contempt.

The door creaked. I saw a piece of white cloth, looming out of the dusk like a moon-flower. It hung from the front of his black cowl, looking for all the world like a torn piece of skin.

Jacques's face glowed a red-black color, from cheek to chin. He didn't recognize me, standing right in front of him, because his glasses had been taken away and he had been brought from the waning sunlight into the darkness. His eyes showed no emotion.

His forehead was bald, just as it had been three years earlier. I might not have recognized him if it weren't for the sparse red hair atop his head. He squatted on the floor with his face down.

The evening wind still blew. The late glow of the sunset—which I could see just a moment before, as a shaft of it flowed in from the window above the sink—was now almost extinct. I sat down in the purple darkness, and looked at Jacques lying on the floor. It was hushed. The lieutenant, Alexandre, and Chavanne had gone off somewhere in the main house to take a coffee break. "It will take the whole night," Alexandre said as he went out of the door.

Jacques groaned very little during the torture. Chavanne beat him first, and then Alexandre; and as I watched, I thought that Jacques would, perhaps, endure it. I waited to see how much his body could take, listening to the sharp, hard sound of the hose as it cut into his flesh. But strangely enough, somewhere in my mind, I prayed for his endurance even as I waited for his screams. On the other hand, if he buckled under the torture, if he gave the names of other liaisons in the sixth arrondissement, as the lieutenant's husky, tender voice invited him to do, then that would mean I had won. It would mean I had proven that one couldn't trust men. Men are so weak, so frail, as to abandon friendship and faith in mankind when faced with physical pain.

Again, the withered trees crackled sharply in the cold beyond the window. Images from three years ago sort of drifted into my mind: Jacques seated next to Marie Thérèse in the classroom; Jacques explaining something to a friend, pointing at a notebook; Jacques and all the other students, sitting in the classroom; their light, youthful laughter; Monique's smile.

Jacques was in convulsions on the floor. I brought a tin of water and poured it, little by little, over his face. I saw blood seeping out, streaking the underwear that protruded from his cowl.

"Ja-a-a-cques," I said in a subdued voice. He opened his eyes; they were hollow, as if the flesh had been scooped out. His bald forehead looked slimy, as if it had been covered with oil. "Jacques, it's me."

Finally he moved his lips. I couldn't tell what he was saying. His tongue sought out the water on his nose and chin, moving about as if it were a living creature. I brought the tin to his lips.

"Do you remember me?" I asked.

Jacques gave a faint nod.

"You do remember me?" I squatted down beside the man, wiped the blood from his face, and again brought the tin of water to his lips. Jacques watched each of my movements with a hollow look, as I attended him. "So you remember me?" I asked again.

He murmured something, panting. I couldn't catch his words.

"What did you say?" I asked, and brought my ear to his lips. "Oh. I got you. It was because I was here that you were able to endure the torture, wasn't it?" I gave a low, wry sort of laugh. I hadn't taken such psychological effects

56

into consideration. But, yes, of course that would make sense.

"Would you like a cigarette?" I took two of my rationed black Gauloises from my pocket and gave one to Jacques. "You hate me that much?"

"No, I don't hate you," he answered in a very faint voice.

"Why did you join the Resistance if you didn't hate me?"

"A Christian doesn't fight out of hatred. He fights for justice."

I scoffed. *For justice?* Jacques again took on the aspect of a man who preached to me in the classroom and knelt in prayer.

Again I heard the limbs of the trees cracking outside the window. I remembered the squeaking sound the lieutenant's boots made earlier as he walked ahead of me over the frozen snow. *I see. Neither Alexandre nor Chavanne should torture Jacques. It has to be me,* I thought. I had to hurry. I had to finish the business before they returned.

"Why are you...?" Jacques murmured. The cigarette in his right hand fluttered slightly.

"Me? I'm investigating students from the University of Lyon who might be involved in the A.S., or in the F.F.I. You know, the Nazis will use any means to achieve their objectives. Even though I'm French, I'm useful to them because I attended the University of Lyon. That's why they hired me."

Jacques cast his small, dark eyes toward me. "*You* hate me, don't you?"

"Yes, I do. Though I assume you knew that before, when we were students."

"Why?" he gasped. "Why do you hate me?"

"Because you want to be a modern-day hero," I said, leisurely lighting a cigarette. Then I reflected. "If you can endure the torture, if you can keep your mouth shut, it's only because you long to be a hero—you are intoxicated by the idea of self-sacrifice. Intoxicated. You get drunk with ideals in order to conquer your fear, and drunk with principles in order to overcome death. The Maquis and you Christians are exactly alike. 'I shoulder all the sins of mankind,' you say. 'I sacrifice my life for the proletariat. I, and I alone, do this.' You are drunk with the pathetic spirit of the martyr. No matter how a Nazi collaborator like me, a traitor, fumbles about with your body, you will never sell your soul as Judas did. That is what you think, isn't it? That's what you believe. You expect too much."

The dusk gradually thickened. It washed over the windows above the sink like a wave and drenched them. I couldn't see anything now but the pale silhouette of Jacques, who remained silent. But I knew how he must look.

"I knew, ever since the old days, that you wanted to be a hero, a martyr. And for that I wanted to knock down your heroic, martyr's face. I thought and thought about it, and now it's clear to me. It's not just you I hate. I hate everyone who is intoxicated with 'belief.' And do you know why? Because they lie. And not only to others. They also lie to themselves.

"Jacques, Nazism is just politics. And politicians know how to strip men of their self-sacrificial heroism. Heroic self-sacrifice can't exist where ego doesn't exist. And ego can be easily shattered. You've heard the story about the Nazi camps in Poland, haven't you? The word is there were a number of stalwart warriors like you in the camps at first—men drunk with martyrdom. And they all waited to be killed *alone*, each by himself, just as you do. Well, sure, because there is a tickling satisfaction in this sublime prospect of a lonely, heroic death. However, Hitler saw through it all. That's why he slaughtered them en masse, as an anonymous bunch of nobodies. He denied them their literary, sentimental end."

I stood up and felt along the wall for the light. A sixty-candle bulb showed Jacques's face clearly, for the first time. It was absolutely without shadow. A face without shadow betrays no emotion. Jacques's face was like a mask, flat and hollow. There was no hatred in it, no pain.

I felt intense rage at this mask. I wanted to shake his face—to distort it. My eyes naturally lit upon Alexandre's hose lying on the floor.

"Do you understand?" I continued. "Solitary, theatrical deaths were the privilege of the condemned up until nineteenth century. The martyrs, those who defied authorities during the Renaissance, the aristocrats at the time of the Revolution: they were granted privilege even in death. But not today. This is the twentieth century, you know. In the twentieth century everything is done en masse. We simply can't afford to grant each of you your heroic death, your artful death."

"But you, too," Jacques hissed, tensely, "you, too, are intoxicated, with evil. You *believe* in it."

"Evil is eternal."

Jacques's hand groped about under his torn-up cowl.

"It will not change in any way," I shouted. I saw a silver metal sparkled amongst his thin, white fingers. It was a cross. It was a cross at the end of a rosary, attached to the inside belt of his cowl.

"It wasn't because I was here that you were able to endure the torture," I said, my whole body quivering. "It was because you were holding the cross, wasn't it? Give the cross to me."

"No!" Jacques shouted, turning toward me a face slimy with blood and sweat.

59

"The cross makes you drunk."

I struck him with my palm. He covered his face with his left hand, holding the cross tightly. Then I cracked the hose. My palm burned as the hose hit him. The sun glared in the skies above Aden. The rock cast its dark shadow over the burnt brown grass. I pushed the boy down. I shoved Jacques down. But it wasn't merely the boy and Jacques I was trampling, beating, cursing, revenging. I was striking out at all of humanity—at everyone who had ever been born into illusion, and died with it. Jacques squirmed over the floor like a caterpillar. His undergarments tore as he rolled about.

"Devil!" he shouted. "You devil!" His pale skin stirred my lust.

"That's enough. We'll do the rest."

I looked back at the voice. The lieutenant, Alexandre, and Chavanne were standing at the door.

"Lieutenant!" I shouted, throwing away the hose. "Let me make him confess."

The lieutenant cast a suspicious look at me.

"There is a girl here called Marie Thérèse. Torture her in front of him." And so I called on Judas again that night.

# Chapter IX

I sat on the edge of the bed. Marie Thérèse inched back like an animal at bay.

Her hand felt for the doorknob. *Click, click*: queer, hard sounds echoed. The knob turned in vain.

Marie Thérèse started to cry, her freckled face wrinkling. She cried like a six- or seven-year-old sweet little girl.

A black cape fell from her shoulders to the floor, as if it were ash crumbling off of her body. I recognized the velvet cape. She had worn it on the night of dance two years ago, the night she chose me instead of Jacques. And tonight she would have to betray Jacques again, simply in order to survive.

I pricked up my ears. But I could hear nothing from the kitchen next door, not even a cough. Had Jacques lost consciousness? Alexandre was to send me a signal if Jacques still refused to confess. And then I would...

Night arrived. I switched on the light. A fly was darting back and forth in the room. A baroque chandelier hung from the ceiling. It must have been the previous owner's taste. The light fell on the mattress, and on the chair with its edges soiled from handling, casting long shadows on the floor. There were several old paintings of Lyon on the wall, depicting men and women at leisure in eighteenth-century costume. The Nazis hadn't touched the interior of the house. Two years ago, this room must have been a guest room, or perhaps the girls' bedroom.

Marie Thérèse sobbed convulsively in the corner of the room, her shoulders shaking.

"I wonder if there isn't some way to put an end to this." I played for time, muttering to myself. "I'm really at a loss. You want to go home, don't you? You know, if only Jacques would tell us the truth, we wouldn't need to hurt either of you." Her sobbing and the fly's buzzing were constant, endless.

The play I had projected, and begun to direct, on the night of the dance two years ago was now approaching its final scene. There is a word: "Providence." It sums up the Christian way of thinking about things unforeseeable, or human fate. Indeed, I never plotted to join the Nazi torturers with whom Jacques and Marie Thérèse were eventually to become entangled. Quite honestly, I thought I left them behind for good when I saw the two praying together at St. Bernard Church that evening. I thought I had abandoned them. But somehow they came back into my life again. I don't know who did it, but it was beyond my will.

As I bit my fingernails, I felt the triangle linking us— Jacques, Marie Thérèse, me—close in, little by little. If Marie Thérèse were to leave this house unharmed, Jacques would have to betray his comrades. He would have to give names and addresses for all the liaisons in the sixth arrondissement. And it would not simply be his comrades that Jacques would betray; he would, at the same time, be turning his back on the cross—the silver cross that hung about his waist.

On the other hand, what did this girl, who was sobbing, wrinkling up her freckled face, have to do with me? If Jacques refused to betray his men, Alexandre and Chavanne would violate her. Jacques must at least know how decisive the effect of that could be on a girl, even if it was forced on her. In the end, both faced, tonight, the dilemma of either betraying or being betrayed. As for me, I would find out whether or not I had defeated Jacques—and not only Jacques, but Christians, revolutionists, Madenier, and Jules Romains as well. All the same, it wasn't me who plucked us up with a pair of tweezers, placed us, like three dolls, on a laboratory table, and then set up this gamble. It wasn't me at all. And if it wasn't me, then who…?

The fly circling the chandelier settled on the wall above the fireplace at last. And all at once a hush descended on the room. The fly folded its wings and rubbed its long front legs, neatly, side to side. I stared at its funny little gesture, still biting my fingernails.

Soon, the fly took off again, this time heading not for the chandelier but for the window that reflected it. The fly struck the glass and fluttered around, as if furious.

And at that moment I saw again, in the windowpane, Jacques' silver cross, the very cross I had seen only minutes before. Yes, I thought I had a vision of it. It struck me that there was something I had missed in sketching out the triangle that linked the three of us. All of a sudden, I became anxious and looked back at Marie Thérèse.

She had stopped crying and lay collapsed at the foot of the door. Her knees touched the floor, and her legs sprawled out, almost in parallel.

Until now, I had known Marie Thérèse only by her thin face, covered with freckles. I never dreamt that she had such straight, shapely legs. Also, her dazzlingly white thighs peeped out from between her upturned skirt and grey socks.

I swallowed. Yvonne's thighs were never as white as

these, when she pinned the old dog down on the street in the Croix Rousse as the wisteria flowers fell. The swatch of Marie Thérèse's thighs that I saw was as pure and white as fresh milk in the morning, and also somehow shy.

I heard myself breathing heavily. And lust wasn't the only thing that overcame me. I felt intense jealousy of this freckle-faced girl for possessing such purity, even if it was only bodily purity. That surely was something I had never had, something of which God had deprived me.

Like a bat with its wings unfurled, my shadow danced from the fireplace to the door when I heard a noise in the kitchen. It was Alexandre's hacking cough. He wrung his throat hard, trying to clear out the phlegm.

"How tenacious you are, Father."

After that, their subdued exchange continued, but I couldn't catch any of it. I stood still, my hand on Marie Thérèse's shoulder. The fly hit the window again and started jerking about, making a dry buzz.

"If you cry out," I said to Marie Thérèse, in a low voice, "Jacques will betray his comrades. If you don't want him to do that, you'll..." My hand touched her trim knee.

Again I heard Alexandre mumble. My fingers crept over Marie Thérèse's knee, like an insect.

A strange voice issued from the kitchen, something between a sigh and a groan. It was the sound of crying! That man, who hadn't uttered so much as a word during one full hour of torture, was crying. *Jacques has broken down!*, I thought vacantly. *Unable to bear the physical pain, he broke down at last, just like any other man. And he is crying and screaming like a baby!*

Hard, rhythmic sounds punctuated each cry, and each time the cry grew higher. It was like an avalanche, taking on speed as it fell. Jacques was falling apart. He was falling apart.

The girl no longer tried to protect herself from me. Her eyes were taut and wide open. Only her knees were shaking. I whispered into her ear. Maybe I said, "It's nothing. Don't be upset!" or something along those lines. I don't recall. I just kept whispering into her ear, as if in a delirium. She stared at me, as emotionless as a doll. I couldn't tell if she was actually listening to me or not.

I do remember, though, that she raised herself up, like a frail patient.

"Please! Please spare her!" Jacques's childish sobs drifted in from the kitchen. "Please, have mercy and let her go!" It stopped abruptly. And then I could hear nothing.

Shortly, I heard the lieutenant's languid voice. "He's fainted. Douse him with water. He'll give it all up this time."

Suddenly, Marie Thérèse began unbuttoning her blouse. At first I didn't understand what she was doing. She knitted her brows painfully and opened the blouse. Then she tried covering herself with her arms.

"Don't beat him. Please don't beat him." Marie Thérèse moved her lips like an idiot.

"What? What did you say?" I drew my ear up close to her. And at that moment, I understood everything. The drama I had imagined, the play I meant to direct, should have been more tragic. But now even this girl wanted to take her part in a farce at the Moulin Rouge. She wanted to play the saint.

I brought my trembling hands to her chest and tore up the blouse. And tore the lacy lingerie that covered her skinny breasts. I had ripped up the lingerie, as soft as sea foam, in that sunny law classroom three years ago. It had been with a different feeling then, but the impulse was essentially the same. Three years ago I didn't really know why I did it, but now I understood. Listening to the crisp sound of her blouse and lingerie as they tore apart in my hands, and looking down at the pained expression of a girl trying to endure, her teeth clenched, I understood for the first time the *meaning*, or say the *mission* if "meaning" sounds odd, of raping a virgin...Water boiled up from the bottom of a bog...*I'm raping. I'm raping!* I groaned....I gritted my teeth. Marie Thérèse didn't exist in my eyes anymore. What I was raping, what I was sullying, was *every* virgin—the illusion of their purity and innocence. Men exist simply to destroy this illusion of purity. Jacques' crucifix was enveloped in an illusion of purity. Concealed there as well were all the stupid dreams, the intoxicating dreams, that Christians, revolutionists, and men like Madenier held out for the future, and for history.

...I was washed away by the waves like a fleck of wood, and swept down to the floor of the sea.

Dead. I have been dead for centuries. The fly was howling, circling around the light.

"Did he faint?"

"No, I think he's just faking it."

Through the wall I could hear the lieutenant and Alexandre whispering. The girl lay beneath me, covering her eyes with her white arm. I put the clothes on her lifeless body. She was as yielding and motionless as a doll, as I lifted her limbs.

"Dead?"

"Yes. I believe so."

I heard the men again, tramping around, pouring water into the tin.

"He chewed up his tongue!" Alexandre shouted.

I ran to the wall and laid my ear against it. I could almost see them, shaking Jacques's body, turning it over.

"I see. He chewed up his tongue!" I said to myself, pressing my head to the wall. I listened as hard, heavy sounds echoed in my head. Before I knew it, I was butting my head against the wall, rhythmically. A weird feeling, an amalgam of sorrow and desolation, oppressed my mind. I had experienced it once before, when I made Marie Thérèse yield to me at the Hotel l'Amour. It was more like profound fatigue than sadness. After filling up the space I had to fill somehow, I didn't know what to do next. *I didn't feel this way at all when I lost my mother!* The feeling might have seemed appropriate if I had lost Jacques, after having loved him for a long time, only to be betrayed by him.

I see. He chewed up his tongue. I really didn't expect it. Suicide was an absolutely unforgivable sin for Catholics. *You are a seminarian. And yet you chose suicide, for which you'll be eternally damned.*

My mild irritation gradually became violent, a storm over a gray sea of sorrow.

*Pointless! It's pointless!* I muttered. *You think you've escaped me by taking your life? You think you've eluded the fate of having to betray your comrades, and determine whether Marie Thérèse lives or dies? Neither the Nazis nor I can use her to hurt you now. But so what? You can't annihilate me. I exist here and now. Suppose I am evil itself. Evil will endure, despite your suicide. Unless you destroy me, your death is pointless. And you know it's pointless.*

Marie Thérèse didn't stir, her arm still covering her face. I couldn't tell if she had heard the business in the kitchen. I merely saw transparent strings of tears as they flowed, little by little, out from under her arm. *It's pointless. Pointless.*

"Jacques is dead," I said to Marie Thérèse, in a brother's tender voice. Her lips trembled, trying to speak.

"Yes? What?" I brought my ear to her lips, but couldn't catch her words. She was singing a song, bringing in a strange melody that somehow sounded delirious, but not delirious.

I was utterly exhausted. My fatigue wasn't merely physical. Nothing could move me anymore.

> *Gather the roses while they're young*
> *Before they wither and fade...*

I had heard the song somewhere before. Yes, it was on the day of the inaugural ceremony at the University of Lyon. But that, too, was pointless now. *She is insane. Marie Thérèse has gone insane*, I thought, listening to her sing. But that didn't move me, either.

Somewhere deep in my head I could hear someone open a door and close it again. "Sonny, my boy." It was my mother calling to me, in the last moment of her life. "Devil!" Jacques had shouted in the hall at the Hotel l'Amour, his fist in the air.

"Right. I'm telling you to look to the RIGHT."

I stood and walked toward the window where that stupid fly had flung itself, hoping to find an escape. It darted about, having a vision of what lay outside. Lyon was burning in the darkness. Bellcoure Plaza, Perache Station, Republique Street, the slope in the Croix Rousse where Yvonne pinned down the dog with her white thighs: all of it had burst into flame. And the flame burned against the dark sky, infinitely.

# YELLOW MAN

In the beginning, God was very lonely in the universe, so he decided to create human beings. He kneaded flour, formed the dough into his own image, and put it into the oven to bake.

He was impatient, though, and opened the door in less than five minutes' time. What he saw, naturally, was a very white man, hardly baked at all.

"Oh well," God muttered to himself. "I will name it White Man."

Edified by this failure, he decided to bake the next man for a longer time. But he dozed off, only to wake up to a burning smell. He jumped toward the oven and opened it. What he saw this time was an over-baked, totally black man.

"What the heck, I will call it Black Man."

At last, God opened the door at the proper time. In the oven, he beheld a man, baked yellow.

"Moderation in all things," God said and nodded. "I will call it Yellow Man."

*—from a fairy tale*

I know thy works, that thou art neither cold nor hot: I would thou wert cold or hot. So then because thou art lukewarm, and neither cold nor hot, I will spew thee out of my mouth.
*—The Revelation of John 3*

# Chapter I

The B29s flew over the Kii Peninsula and then disappeared into the ocean, at dusk. Now, the hush is uncanny, so quiet that it's hard to credit the hell on earth that the bombing made only two hours ago. The black flames that licked over the Kawanishi Aircraft Factory are now extinguished, though I can still feel dull bangs through the cracked window, if only faintly, from whatever it is that's exploding. Itoko is asleep in bed, like a corpse. Actually, I'm not sure if she really is sleeping. A silky red string of blood runs from her cheek to her mouth. And I don't feel like wiping it away. The way I feel, it would be all right even if she *were* dead.

Father, I'm writing this letter by the light of a stubby candle, not knowing if it will reach you in the camp in Takatsuki. But I will continue, anyway. Mr. Durand is dead. And before he died, he asked me to give you his diary, which I am enclosing with this letter.

My weary heart felt not the slightest shock, nor any horror, when I heard of Mr. Durand's death. Now, I feel it was like listening to the distant sounds of winter winds, that it had been decided years ago that he was to die. So many die these days that death seems natural. And, reading the diary the old man left me, all I can think is, *I see—so it is. But that has nothing to do with me.* I suppose it's not entirely right to say it has *nothing* to do with me, as the diary mentions you and me on almost every page. But, yellow man that I am, I read it as though it belonged to a

71

strange, distant world. Never had I imagined that our yellow world could so agitate that old man, or stir up such envy inside him. However, I feel neither responsibility nor satisfaction when I think about the color of my skin. White men like you and Mr. Durand can make tragedies, or comedies, out of life. But for me there is no drama. And I didn't lose it somewhere along the way. It has been like that from the beginning, ever since I was a boy, and even then I was already fooling you.

Father, you never doubted I was an innocent and ignorant boy. Just remember the little boy that I was, reciting his lines at mass every Sunday morning, confessing his sins, stammering in the little confessional. But I didn't know what sin was. Or I should say, I didn't have a sense of guilt. I just believed it was my Christian duty to confess my sins. So I made up stories of having been lazy at school, or of having heard dirty stories from friends, or whatever. You would prick your ears to catch my frightened voice in that dark little closet with its coarse cotton screens shutting out the light and noise from outside.

"Minoru-san, state it briefly," you would say. "What did you do?"

Through the lattice, I breathed in your white-man's breath, which smelled of butter and wine mixed together. I sighed, tired out by the unnatural business forced on me.

That confessional comes to mind as I write this letter.

*State it briefly*...I know! I'm trying to write briefly about how cold last winter was, about the night I saw Mr. Durand, and about the morning you were taken away and turned over to the special political police in Nishinomiya. But those incidents, though less than three months old, are like dead leaves, now, at the bottom of a marsh, all but indistinguishable from the mud. If I try to pluck them up, one by one, they will fall apart, leaving fragments of debris in my palm.

Father, I can't help thinking that, after all, our karma, or our sin, isn't the sort of thing that might be so easily cataloged and classified as it typically is in your confessional. I hope you don't conclude, in the white man's way of thinking, that I write this letter tonight out of some urge to repent of my sins, because I'm overcome by emptiness, and because I can't help but pray over the sad plight of humanity. Let me repeat: As a yellow man, I know nothing so grave, or so dramatic, as your sense of sin, or your "emptiness." All I know is fatigue. Deep fatigue. A fatigue as cloudy as my yellowish skin, and as dank and sunken.

I don't know when the fatigue set in. I can say, though, that just as dust incrementally accumulates on tables and bookshelves, something—something like a thin membrane—started to cover my eyes about three years ago. Probably you remember. I went home to Nigawa and visited your church in the summer of the year before last—the year I entered medical school in Yotsuya. You seemed to notice this membrane over my eyes. You stared at me, anxiously.

"You attend mass regularly in Tokyo, don't you?" you asked. "Science by no means conflicts with religion. Many in France are both honored medical doctors and Christians in good standing..."

I smiled weakly, listening to your smattering of Japanese. The red flowers of sweet-scented oleanders were in bloom in the churchyard. I heard the children reciting their catechism together, led by Aya-san, the missionary.

"What are the ten commandments of God?"

"The ten commandments of God are..."

When I was a child, you taught me about God and made me recite his commandments. You were still young. The red

73

flowers of oleanders were blossoming then, too. The Roman collar of your black cassock was snow white.

"Christ was born in a stable. He was poor." You looked us over with your moist, brown eyes, and opened a large, illustrated Bible. And at that moment, I learned, for the first time, that God was a white man with blond hair—just like you.

"Is God a foreigner?" I asked.

"No," you said, shaking your head resentfully. "God isn't a man. He knows no nationality."

But, Father, you were wrong. Indeed, I stopped attending mass once I moved to Tokyo. But it wasn't, as you had worried, because of some earth-shattering paradox, like the contradiction between medical science and religion, or the unscientific nature of God's existence. Actually, I really didn't care about those very Western sorts of debate, which all earnest young Christians have to survive.

I was tired that summer. Not just physically. Somehow my mind was exhausted, too. I simply didn't have the stomach to digest this white man—this Christ with blond hair and blond beard, as shown in your illustrated Bible.

One morning, about four months earlier, I suffered a fit of coughing in my room in Sendagaya. A small amount of bloody sputum came up. I had my chest X-rayed. There was a whitish cavity, about two centimeters in diameter, in my left lung.

"It's a case of pleural adhesion, so we can't perform a pneumothorax." My senior at the school, an assistant, murmured as if to himself, as he reviewed my case in the lab. He stared at the floor, avoiding looking at me. "But you'll be all right. Just take a leave of absence from school and get some rest in the countryside. And, hey, congratulations! You've escaped the draft!" He forced out a laugh.

I knew he wasn't telling me the truth. Food rations being what they were, you couldn't even take in the nutrition necessary to fight off my disease. As I listened to the assistant, absently, my thoughts wandered. *Will I have another six or seven years to live, if I'm lucky?* Weak, early-winter sunlight shone through the broken windowpane of the laboratory, scattering across a floor littered with tubes. Strangely, death seemed neither terrifying nor close.

In late fall of that year, the war grew worse and worse. Every night a formation of B29s materialized out of the southern ocean, looking like white sesame seeds. They flew over Tokyo and then vanished, burning up district after district. As medical students, we spent every morning carrying out the dead, or sitting by waiting for air-raid victims to breathe their last.

Standing at Yotsuya-mitsuke on a sunny winter day we could overlook a barren stretch of land extending from Hanzomon to Ginza, with nothing but scorched utility poles and collapsed walls scattered about. The wind would raise a yellowish cloud of dust under the leaden sky. People wandered about the ruins with their heads down, dragging their feet at every step.

I didn't care anymore whether or not we won the war. I felt nothing beyond a mere registration of facts, even when I heard that friends had been killed here, or lost there. As the hospital had burned down, the medical school found temporary classrooms, with broken windows. And, sitting in those classrooms, I sometimes pictured you riding your bike along the white path in Nigawa heading to Takarazuka to do missionary work. That is to say, I pictured your clean, snow-white collar, you who were able to give the mass, to hear confessions, to solace the sick, and to work for his religion and for his mission. But even that white collar gradually faded, and eventually disappeared, as the gray membrane settled over my eyes.

One morning, about a week after I'd coughed up that blood-stained sputum, I stepped off the train at Shinano-machi station to go to school. A compulsory evacuation had been ordered just recently for the area behind the station. Weak, winter-morning sun shone over the premises, which were buried under the rubble. I noticed an old man in khaki work clothes crouching in the middle of the debris, seated with his back toward me.

The sun fell weakly on his bony back. The clean, white bag of a survival kit lay at his feet.

I passed through the evacuated area again that evening, on my way home from the lectures. A few workmen stood about, their arms crossed, with a policeman in their midst, all buffeted by the yellowish wind. I noticed a straw mat spread over the rubble, with a bulge in it. A pair of feet in tattered shoes protruded from under the mat.

I approached a man who stood there watching, leaning against a bicycle by the road. "What happened?"

"It seems an old guy fell dead on the street. It's a case of malnutrition, obviously. Looks like that's all he possessed." The man pointed at a tree still standing amid the rubble, thoroughly scorched. The white bag hung from a blackened limb, swinging languidly in the wind.

Somehow, the scene provoked in my mind an image of an old beast that leaves his herd, and who wanders around a grove or a marsh, alone, looking for a place to lay its body down. And I thought, "I want to settle down somewhere in Nigawa, quietly and peacefully, like this old man..."

76

Nigawa was devastated...

Compared to other residential areas in Hanshin like Ashiya or Mikage, Nigawa has drier air and whiter soil, and takes on something of the aspect of a small, exotic village. This is owing to Mt. Kabutoyama, a round, extinct volcano, and to the granite hill that surrounds it. The Nigawa River, a branch of the Mukogawa, starts its journey on this mountain. Maybe that is why the Canadians, so far away from their mother land, chose the site when they founded, around 1932, a school called Kansei Gakuin. They settled in a cream-colored, Western-style house they built in a grove of Japanese red pines, and planted the colorful cosmos flowers that bloom in autumn.

Your Catholic church was located on the other side of the river from this Protestant school. Much later, those who couldn't afford a house in Ashiya or Mikage vied with one another to build houses between those two Christian outposts, taken in by the advertisements of the Hankyu Railway, and of a home builder considered trendy in those days. They were typically semi-Western houses, with a veneer of luxury that had great appeal to upstart social climbers.

As I got off at the station on the Hankyu line, for the first time in two years, I tried without success to find my boyhood in the landscape of Nigawa. I'm not thinking about the hours I spent in the red-pine forests, or on the white granite hills. I have in mind the exotic landscape that Nigawa had craftily fabricated, while remaining unmistakably a part of Japan. After all, it was very much like me, who had been born yellow, and was forced into a christening, by my mother and my aunt, at your church.

The town, however, had assumed the empty look of an old man's face, now that the war had necessitated the

77

Canadians' departure. The river had been filled in to use as cropland, and the cream-colored building, which had once housed the Canadians, became a dormitory for factory workers. The red-pine forest had been cut down for use in the production of airplane fuel. And, at dusk, you couldn't look at the riverbank without seeing men walking along, feet dragging, wearily shouting out military songs.

"Who are they?" I asked our family's old retainer.

"Conscript laborers. They work at the Kawanishi Factory."

As he said, a factory belonging to Kawanishi Aircraft, painted in camouflage, had been built over what used to be a golf course that stretched all the way to Takarazuka. Every morning and evening, the tiny railroad station over-flowed with Kansei Gakuin students wearing oil-stained work clothes, or loose work pants. Even the students from Itoko's St. Mary's Women's School mingled among them.

"All the foreigners are gone?"

"Except for the Father and Mr. Durand. Just the two of them now."

"Well, Nigawa might be the next target of the B29s."

"Right. It's good your mother and sisters already evac-uated. Really."

What I wanted was to be in some quiet place, where I didn't have to think of air raids or corpses. If I had to die of tuberculosis anyway, I wanted to do it without the distur-bance of all the hellfire and noise. But it was hardly likely that this town, which the foreigners had abandoned, and which now had its grotesque factory, would escape the bombing, now that even Itami had been attacked.

I decided to go help my uncle at his hospital in Kotoen twice a week. It wasn't so I could get the treatment I needed. I did it because otherwise I would've been conscripted or compelled into labor of some kind or another. The rest of the week, I just lay quietly in a room of the empty, dusty house, which had no furniture left in it, without going to church or visiting you.

Itoko was the only one who visited me now and then. As you know, Itoko is my cousin. When I came back two years ago, I made love to her for the first time. I just wanted to turn away from the dark times. The still stiff, but fresh, white body of this St. Mary's Women's School student somehow didn't have the smell of death.

But today she'd changed, just as Nigawa changed. Itoko and her classmates had been ordered to wash the coarse work clothes of the factory hands at Kawanishi, day after day. Blood oozed from her chapped hands. Her fingers were all cracked. She wore work pants instead of the fluffy white uniform of St. Mary's, and her hair was up in a bun at the back, like that of a peasant's wife. I don't believe I have to tell you that Itoko is Saeki's fiancé. You know, Saeki and I served as altar boys at your church when we were children. And I better not say why Itoko betrayed this pious young man. He was in the army at Tsu city in Mie at the time.

Out of sheer inertia, I continued to force myself on Itoko, burdening my emaciated shoulders all the more with a severe fatigue. I felt no guilt, no pang of conscience. True, I was sorry for Saeki. But I felt as if I were rolling down a long, dark slope, and couldn't do anything to stop it.

I made love to Itoko in my room again that evening. Low, heavy clouds had covered the sky in the afternoon, and it looked like it might snow at any moment. Through the window, I glanced out at the yard, which was scruffy with neglect. The stems of the cannas and the cockscombs, which my sisters had planted years ago, stuck out of the ground like reddish brown bones. Some week-old snow remained, grimy, in a shady corner along the hedge. Placing my lips over Itoko's, I stared blankly at the medal of the Virgin Mary that hung from her neck.

In the gray haze of evening, Itoko's face showed faintly white, like a moonflower. She also was gazing into the desolate yard, eyes wide open, and with a shadowy pain between her eyebrows. I remember how she would close her eyes and give a small whimper as I caressed her. *I wonder if she, too, is thinking about death*, I asked myself. And strange though it may be, Father, death didn't terrify us, or seem, in prospect, hideous. I didn't know whether it was love or lust that led me to force myself on Itoko. As I say, I had no feelings of guilt or fear. It was simply that I would continue to sleep with Itoko, as my body grew further and further enervated, until I died, and there was nothing I could do about it. Grim resignation proved stronger than the Christian doctrine you taught me.

"I wonder what'll become of us," Itoko murmured, in an absent voice.

"Well, I don't know."

"I wonder how long the war will last."

"It *will* end someday. But it makes little difference when."

"Right. I guess it doesn't."

Itoko raised her tired, blemished face and stared at me. Then she sat up in slow motion, like a doll, and held the medal of the Virgin in her hand. I heard the radio coming from the shack where the old retainer and his wife lived. It was broadcasting the movements of an enemy airplane, which was circling to the south of Wakayama.

"It's strange," I said. "Come to think of it, you're engaged to Saeki. That makes what we are doing immoral."

80

"Oh, stop it," Itoko said, languidly getting out of bed. She sat in the corner, and pulled on her slacks. "Just stop it."

"Do you still see Father Breau? Do you attend mass?"

"Only occasionally. But I don't care anymore whether or not God exists."

The winds started to blow. I heard something pop out in the copse toward the back.

I walked with Itoko to the station on the Hankyu line. She huddled herself up in an overcoat, an air-raid hood covering her head.

*I don't care anymore whether or not God exists.* After Itoko boarded the train with its blackout curtains drawn, I thought of the medal on her chest. *That's right. Nothing matters. And anyway, the Blessed Virgin doesn't live in our country.* Ice-cold winds blew down from Mt. Kabutoyama, skating over the surface of the river. Every one of the houses along the river had been darkened, preparing for the warnings. It had been two months since I came back to Nigawa. But I hadn't visited you or your church. I wasn't willing to have a hollow conversation with you, who would naturally assume I was still a Catholic, just as you had done two years ago. A tiny star twinkled faintly in a rift in the clouds, fighting against the fierce winds. The pine trees behind Nigawa Bridge rustled, making a melancholy sound. I was running a slight fever, as I always did after forcing myself on Itoko.

A long time ago, when I was a boy, Itoko and I often played "make-believe" in the forest: we would be the Holy Family. Itoko was Mary, I was Joseph, and her celluloid Kewpie doll was the baby Jesus. One of the old burial mounds scattered around here served as the stable, the site of the nativity, where the Magi came. Inside the mound, where the ancient people lay buried together with their clay figures, the rotting stones and soil gave off the sweet smell of death. "I'm scared," Itoko would say, clinging to me. "There are house centipedes here." But I felt a mysterious lure in the darkness of the mound. Even though I was just a child, I sensed a pagan tranquility you could never know— a complete freedom from the terror of death, from fear of sin, and from eternal damnation in hell.

"We can't walk *that* way," said Itoko. Her soft cheeks smelled of the strawberries and cream she'd eaten for lunch. "Mr. Durand's house is there. He's going to hell, you know. Mom told me so."

Father, the night I walked Itoko to the station, Mr. Durand's small house was freezing out among the pines in the jet-black darkness, where the winds swirled after blowing down, fiercely, off Mt. Kabutoyama. *He's going to hell.* As Itoko's remark implied, all the church members in Nigawa believed it, including my mother and my aunt. I remember, when I was a child, finding the signature of Father Durand on my baptismal certificate. "Oh. Mr. Durand baptized me," I said to my mother. "So that means he's a priest?"

"Stop it," my mother replied, turning her sour face away. "Anyway, you are *not* to talk to that foreigner."

Years later I learned that this old foreigner with tar-stained whiskers and a bald head had been a Catholic priest. Though he was supposed to be celibate, he had a liaison with a Japanese woman and was expelled from the church. On special occasions like feasts, this apostate would hide himself behind a column of the chancel, like a homeless beggar, and attend mass. And after the congregation left the building, he would leave from the back gate, like an outcast.

"He's a disgrace to the Catholic church. Seriously, thanks to him, *we* get suspicious looks." The congregation criticized you behind your back for letting that Judas into their church. "Even Father Breau is defiled," they said.

Children used to ambush the old fellow as he left the church, and limped his way back to Nigawa Bridge, dragging his rheumatic legs. They "stoned him with stones," from behind, literally executing the commands of the Bible.

"I'm an old man. Please spare me!" Mr. Durand would cry, in the midst of a shower of pinecones and rocks, supporting his body with a stick and covering his face with his right hand. And then he disappeared into the forest, the cruel children's whoops of triumph pelting his back.

I thought of that as I squatted down to pick up a pinecone just like the one I once threw at Mr. Durand. It was dry and had opened up. I held it in my palm and sniffed it—the smell of sin and soil. "Innocent childhood" is a fairy-tale told by grown-ups. How many times had I thrown these pinecones and broken the windowpanes of the house that now stood before my eyes? The cruel, eight-year-old boy I had been hadn't felt the slightest compassion for the old fellow. To rid the congregation of that sinner, to cast that apostate out, as Christ had expelled the money-changers from the temple: I thought this would be the proof of my faith.

The shutters were closed tightly. I couldn't hear a thing. Some rush mats and a stick for beating out fires lay in front of the gate. I could easily picture the old fellow being hauled out for an air-raid drill and shoved about by rowdies from the defilade squad. The apostate is probably inside the house, totally shut in, with the lights switched off. And, holding his breath, he might well be rubbing his tar-stained whiskers against his mistress at this very moment. They are like Itoko and me, simply waiting to waste away with emaciation, until death seizes them. In a flash, a pain shot through my chest. *I am an old man. Please spare me.* I could almost hear his hangdog voice. I crushed the pinecone in my palm, feeling a hot pain.

A flashlight shone on my face, from behind a utility pole.

"Why, you aren't even wearing gaiters. Don't you know they've issued a warning?"

I couldn't see a face, as he had turned off the light immediately.

"You a student?" I don't know why, but he lowered his voice. "Show me your student ID."

"I've come to see Mr. Durand." I swallowed, bracing myself. "On an errand."

"Errand? What sort of errand?"

"I'm learning French from him."

"You are studying a foreigner's language while your nation is in crisis!" He spat onto the ground hatefully and released my arm, which he had been holding in a tight grip. "If you ever do...you'll never get away with it..."

I caught his words in fragments through the wind. When he freed my body, my face was as hot as if somebody had slapped it. I could feel his eyes boring into my back as I walked up to Mr. Durand's door. I had no other choice but to ring the bell.

# Chapter II

## DURAND'S DIARY

### DECEMBER 5TH

I felt, as I feel every morning, that the path from my house to the church seems much longer coming back than it does going out.

As always, I was thoroughly chilled by the time I left the church. I buried my face in the scarf Kimiko knit for me out of her sweater, and walked down the street. The week-old snow had frozen, and gleamed in the darkness. The whole town still lay sleeping, hushed. When I reached Nigawa Bridge, the icy winds off Mt. Kabutoyama hit my face with terrible force. My heart being weak, I had to rest there for a spell, leaning against the stone railing and burying my face in my hands. There again I saw it clearly in my closed eyes, my face as it would be when I was dead. It was the death mask of a man who was bound for hell.

When I was a priest, I often attended my parishioners on their deathbeds. The late Mr. Domoto, or Mrs. Saito, or Ayuko-chan "Theresia, the Little Flower," whom I most doted on in those days. I was the one who gave them extreme unction. Apart from a hint of the affliction of earthly life, which floated about their eyes like a dark sea, their faces were embraced by the tranquility of a Sabbath that is utterly beyond the living, once they commended their souls to the Most High.

My face, in my vision at the bridge, wasn't like that at all. The death mask I saw was like that of Judas, who betrayed Christ and hanged himself. It was...

*I really should stop*...I decided to keep this notebook in the strongbox, lest Kimiko should find it, together with that Browning pistol.

Kimiko was out in the kitchen, preparing supper. I stared for a while at this object which I obtained five years ago to kill myself with, like Judas. It shone heavy and dull in the winter-evening sunlight, which came in, aslant, through the window. The muzzle was like the sunken, hollow eye-socket of an old man. In that humid, Japanese summer, Kimiko and I became slaves to a horrifying lust. The hoarse croaks of frogs came in through the window. When we finished the business, I came back to the vicarage and, with my face buried in the damp bedding, applied the muzzle to my temple, again and again. My finger quivered and did not bend. I could not die.

With the secret help of my friend Father Breau, I continue like a living corpse, hiding myself from the congregation.

## DECEMBER 8TH

"And if thy hand offend thee, cut it off: it is better for thee to enter into life maimed, than having two hands to go into hell, into the fire that never shall be quenched."

I, a priest from France, had committed adultery in Japan, where I had come to do missionary work! The story spread quickly all over this small town on the outskirts of Takarazuka. Several members left the church because of the incident. And I was excommunicated. This sin would affect not merely the sinner. I had deserted the flock of sheep that the Lord had entrusted to me, here in the midst of wilderness and woods, not through indolence but through betrayal. "And whosoever shall offend one of these little ones that believe in me, it is better for him that a millstone were hanged about his neck, and he were cast into the sea."

I know it. No matter what Father Breau may say to console me, I will burn in the fire that shall never be quenched.

Lord, I don't understand you anymore. You toy with me, destroy me, and for all I know you amuse yourself by doing it. Now I feel that I can picture the chilling look on your face when you spoke to Judas at the Last Supper: "That thou doest, do quickly." If Judas was one of your disciples, if he was one of the men for whom you were to be lashed and crucified, if he was one whom you died in order to save—then why did you thus abandon him?

"Judas, I offer my hand to you, too. There is no sin in my book for which you will not be forgiven. My love is infinite." This you did not say. All that the Bible recorded were these terrible words of yours: "It had been good for that man if he had never been born."

*If I had never been born*: From the bottom of my heart I wish it, together with Judas. And now, when it is impossible for me to be born again, God forbids me to kill myself.


## DECEMBER 9TH

After the mass, I hid myself behind the door of the church, and waited for the congregation to leave. With the onset of winter, the number of people who attended the daily morning mass had significantly decreased. The stalwart members, though, the people I had christened long ago—Miss Ishida, Ayako-san, the Missionary and teacher at the Catholic kindergarten, Mrs. Shimamura, Mrs. Ishii—they remained for some time in front of the church, chatting in subdued voices. No doubt they had noticed I was there, because it was obvious that they were pretending not to see me.

"The detective from Nishinomiya came again yesterday afternoon," said Ayako-san to Miss Ishida. She wore work pants, a black sweater, and a pair of rimless glasses, over which she stole a glance at me. She turned her eyes away and continued with a coolly apathetic look. "Well, he came up to me and spoke viciously, saying things like 'Do you Christians trust the Emperor, or do you serve a Western people's God?' Or, 'After all, there are two Westerners at the head of this church. Who knows what you all are up to, under a pretext of Christian worship?'"

"'Who knows what we are up to'?" Miss Ishida repeated, tapping her foot in agitation. "What does that mean? The detective isn't saying we're unpatriotic, is he? That's why I've kept saying we should hold a mass for the fallen soldiers."

"Oh, not that, Ishida-san. The police meant—" At that, Ayako-san held her tongue. She cast a glance at me again, then drew herself up close to Mrs. Shimamura and Miss Ishida. She whispered at their ears, "Well, they were thinking of that shameless—"

I closed my eyes and called out to Kimiko in my mind. She was only thirty. But what with fetching food and moonlighting, she already had a crook in her back, like an elderly woman. Now that I could no longer depend on God, I couldn't leave Kimiko—even if she *was* to be my companion in hell.

(That night, as the cold muzzle touched my forehead in

the dead silence of the room, I felt a force, as if from without, desperately trying to hold my arm down. Stop, stop! Don't do it! It might all be well enough for you. But what about Kimiko? You can die anytime you wish, but that's..." And, coward that I am, I gave in to the temptation.)

The chat came to an end and they dispersed. The sky was gray, just as it was yesterday. It looked like it would snow later. My heart started to ache again.

I crouched like a beast, and stayed out for quite a while. It is exactly twelve years to the day since I left France for the church in Sakase.

When I came to the town of Nigawa in 1933, determined to devote my life to missionary work, the Hankyu Railway had only lately begun parceling its land out in lots, as a new residential area of suburban Hanshin. There wasn't much more than a grocer and tobacco shop in front of the station, together with a field office of the housing corporation. The church with its belfry was not yet there. Neither was the vicarage Father Breau lives in now. I myself obtained, with the permission of the Bishop, all those objects in the chancel, the silver candle holder, the statue of St. Joseph, and so on, from my hometown of Lyon. The small farmhouse I rented became at once my church, the kindergarten in which I taught the catechism to the peasants' children, and my vicarage.

The site of that house must be right where I was crouching, near the entrance to the church.

I stroked the ground like a child, with my freezing fingers. Instantly, my eyes filled with tears—tears issuing from somewhere between regret and bitterness.

When I raised my face, Breau was gazing sadly down at me, his hands in the sleeves of his black cassock. He knew what that day meant to me.

"Pierre, you'll get chilled. Have a cup of hot tea in my room before you head home. Besides, I have something to give you."

He nudged my shoulder and urged me into the vicarage.

Again, I accepted it—one of the hundred yen notes Breau has secretly been giving me for the past eight years. (He said the bishop sent it to me through him, but I knew that wasn't true.) I know Breau takes this precious money from his own private savings. I have no choice but to accept it. Without the money, Kimiko and I could not even buy a slice of bread.

"I heard the police came," I said. I broached the subject to conceal my embarrassment, and to save him a little pain.

"Oh." Breau clicked his tongue and sank into his thoughts, stirring the tea. This man was my junior in the seminary. He has put on the years, too. He is not even fifty yet, but his temples are streaked with gray, and his hollow eyes have dark circles around them. "They've also been to St. Mary's Women's School in Obayashi, many times. I made a phone call the day before yesterday and learned that the Italian Sisters had been taken in to the police in Takatsuki. They are going to be sent somewhere, it seems."

"How about the French?" My tone was frightened.

Breau stole a reproachful glance at me.

"Don't worry. You'll be all right. You have Japanese citizenship."

In his eyes I saw the unmistakable sign of contempt for my despicable cowardice, as he stood up and saw me off at the door.

Standing on Nigawa Bridge on the way home, I covered my face with my hands and thought about my future, just as I did four days ago. It was not cowardice alone that made me say what I said to Father Breau. I have to think about Kimiko. Suppose I was taken away by the Japanese police? How would she get along? If I was alone, like Father Breau...But then I realized again what a hypocrite I was. I had sowed the seeds of evil myself. I couldn't bear to be alone even eight years ago. The devil made use of that sentiment called "pity" in order to trap Kimiko and me—a priest—into committing the mortal sins of adultery, lust, and sacrilege.

## DECEMBER 10TH

All day I thought about that word "pity," which I inscribed here just last night. Kimiko is gone to scavenge for food in the village of Miyake, beyond Takarazuka. She had heard about a farmer who was selling rice and vegetables under the table. Needless to say, she is going to pay for the food with the one hundred yen note Father Breau gave me yesterday.

I had a frugal lunch without Kimiko. Then I brought a chair out onto the verandah, and sat there until the sun went down.

Is it true that I approached Kimiko solely out of pity?

It happened on September 11th, 1937. I still remember going out, in spite of the rain, to visit Father Houssin at his church in Mikage. When night fell, I thought of going home, but the rain that started at dusk was now a heavy downpour. The radio was announcing a severe storm. I was a little anxious about my church in Nigawa. I tried to phone, but the line was already dead. All the trains had been stopped. So, having no other choice, I stayed with Father Houssin that night. There were no lights of course. As I looked out of the window, I saw a muddy stream swirling around his church. The Father, an old missionary couple, and myself huddled together in one room, prepared for the worst.

It was still raining the next morning. Every street was now a swirling muddy stream. But the houses around the church seemed to have escaped harm, so we persuaded each other that the storm had not been so fierce after all. We had been in Japan for four or five years, and were used to the typhoons of autumn.

I took my leave a little after noon, when the sky cleared, though Father Houssin tried to dissuade me. With a light heart and barefoot, I made my way back through the muddy water, which had started to recede. But the Hanshin Railroad had not been reopened yet. Not only that, the bulletin board indicated that they had no prospect of resuming the service.

"Haven't you heard? Forget about the trains!" A station employee bawled at me, as if he were furious. Then I learned what was up. He told me that Sumiyoshi was not so badly damaged, but most of the houses from Uozaki to Ashiya had been buried under mudslides from the Rokko Mountains. A terrific number of people had been swallowed up in the muddy floods.

"Do you see that mountain? *That* one?"

Still dubious, I looked at the Rokko Mountains, toward which the station employee was pointing. In the clearing, blue sky of autumn, the cluster of mountains stood with its blood-colored earth exposed down one side, where not a single tree, nor any grass, remained.

"Everything was flooded," the man said. "And it flowed in this direction, you know. All the houses are gone."

I rolled up my pant legs and walked again, barefoot. As I drew closer to the village of Uozaki, I stopped repeatedly to look around. Roofs and the tips of utility poles peeked out of yellow water. Rice paddies and farmland had become a mere expanse of brown mud, now that the floods were subsiding. Such was the damage wrought by the floods and winds of 1937.

Two days later I met Kimiko. I walked from Ashiya to Uozaki again, asking after the Japanese parishioners who lived in that area.

The damage along the Ashiya and the Sumiyoshi Rivers was particularly bad. Houses had been completely buried by the sands washed down from the upper reaches of the rivers. The trunks of big trees, and huge rocks, had piled up on top of them. Bare-chested junior high school students in khaki pants were pulling on ropes to remove them.

Fragments of clothing, old shoes, even dolls, protruded from the mud under the intense sun.

I saw an old man sitting, with a dazed, spiritless look on his face, on top of what used to be a part of his house. But what made the whole thing so sad was the constant droning of the cicada that had settled on his back.

Kimiko had gazed at my face blankly, sitting on a rock just like the old man. I asked her for directions. But she just shook her head; she hadn't the energy to answer.

"You need food?" I asked, approaching her. "Are you sick?"

And this was Kimiko. At a stroke, she had lost both parents and her sister in the floods three days ago. She alone survived, clinging to a sewing machine as she was swept away.

I asked her if she had some relatives she could turn to. Kimiko shook her head again.

"How about money?"

She did not have that, either. She said she was staying at an elementary school that the town office had designated. I gave her a tiny sum of money and the address of my church in Nigawa, and told her to visit me if things got worse.

I believed in myself back then. I believed in my duty, and in my strength, as a priest. In age, Kimiko and I were more than twenty years apart. I had already reached the time of life that the French call "the Age of Enlightenment." To an aging man like me, she was like a daughter. Father Pinay says that the devil shows himself best when people forget he even exists. And since the flood, he had shrewdly made use of this Pierre Durand's good intentions, pride, and sense of duty. Christ is not the only one who could work the Miracle of Cana. The devil knows how to turn wine into poison.

In those days, Aunt Tami, the housekeeper who waited on me hand and foot, had been telling me that she wanted to take a leave of absence. Her son had been sent to the front, so her daughter-in-law had to work their farm, leaving no one to take care of the children.

It was dusk, three days after we had met in Uozaki, that Kimiko turned up, out of the blue, at my church, like an apparition. (I still remember it. I stepped out of the building after benediction, and there she was, in the gray haze of evening. She was leaning against the gate, a hollow expression on her face, holding a bundle wrapped in cloth in her arms.) I was utterly bewildered. I did not mean that I would take her in, when I gave her the address of my church. Such an undertaking properly belonged to the first-aid station, or to the Department of Welfare of the prefecture.

Anyhow, I remonstrated with Aunt Tami, but she was adamant that I grant her a leave. And, taking pity on Kimiko, she had allowed the girl to stay, without my permission, in her little hut, which stood just off from my house. Kimiko lived with Aunt Tami for about a week, cleaning the church and attending to the chicken house.

I thought things would work out, somehow. It was a big mistake. As Aunt Tami finally set out for her home in the village of Obayashi, she whispered to me.

"Father, Kimiko's got a little one in her tummy."

"Little one?"

"Yes. A baby. You haven't noticed?"

It had been careless of me not to notice the subtle changes in Kimiko's body. She had told me about her parents and sister, but not a word about the pregnancy. I had known nothing about *that*. I couldn't afford to accommodate her at the church any longer.

Some women in the church started to turn against Kimiko. Like ants communicating by sense of smell to find a distant source of food, they found out about Kimiko's past in no time. According to the rumors, Kimiko used to be the maid of a Turkish trader in Kobe. And this Turk had made her pregnant.

"Father, how long are you going to keep that tramp here?"

When pressed like this by Mrs. Shimamura, by Mrs. Ishii, and by Ayako-san the nurse, I felt intense fury toward them, as I always had. They belong to the tribe of that Levite who abandoned the sick, as described in the Gospel of Luke.

"Kimiko-san is pregnant," I declared before I knew it. "I can't just throw her out."

I can't deny that it chilled my relations with the congregation. I was compelled to send Kimiko off to live with Aunt Tami.

I still remember every instant of that dreadful night.

When I told Kimiko to leave, she just nodded without any expression.

"Be ready by evening," I said. And when she waited on

95

me at supper, I asked, "Do you know where Aunt Tami's house is?"

"She drew a map for me," came the languid reply.

I went back to my room after supper and started to put the church accounts in order, my pipe in my mouth. Kimiko remained awhile in the kitchen doing the dishes. Then it seemed she went back out to the hut.

It struck me as odd when Kimiko had not come to take her leave, even after two hours passed. I put on sandals and went out to the hut, flashlight in hand. I knocked on the door. Silence. I cracked open the door and saw Kimiko lying face down on the tatami mat. A box of sleeping pills was next to her.

I remember that the night was extremely close. As it did on those uneasy nights that follow the rainy season, the humidity peculiar to Japan now saturated the steamy room. Frogs, which I detest, were croaking all around the church. A brown moth struck the dim thirty-watt bulb as it flew around, scattering white powder. I sat at Kimiko's side and wiped her small forehead, where a few stray hairs were pasted. She lay asleep, with her mouth slightly open. (But was she *really* asleep at that moment?) I looked down at her face. As is always the case with Japanese women, Kimiko's small, flat face had neither shadow nor depth. No emotion was expressed on it, no grief, no hatred—nothing.

*O Lord, this forlorn woman...*

But she was not really forlorn. I couldn't see in her face what we Europeans like to describe as despair or alienation—that theatrical, warped sort of darkness. Nevertheless, I could imagine nothing more distant from God than the impassive, Noh-mask face of this Oriental woman.

I felt stifled as I gazed at her face in a room full of the odor of the sick. I stood to open the window and let in some fresh air. Then Kimiko pulled the comforter up to her neck and stared at me with long, narrow eyes...

I was in a stupor when it was over. The croak of the frogs became particularly intense for a while. The moth fell onto the tatami mat with a plop. It lay dead on its back, showing its plump, silver belly. And the room was saturated with the hot, sticky air. I—

I had to set the diary aside.

Kimiko had not yet returned from her shopping expedition. And it was nearly eight o'clock. I grew anxious. I closed the notebook and went out to meet her at Nigawa station on the Hankyu line.

I locked the house and went out. Black winds swirled in the pine grove. I buried my face in the scarf, and carefully stepped along the riverbank so as not to slip on the icy streets, dragging my rheumatic legs. I waited by the ticket gate until a little past nine, exposed to the chilly winds that blew across the river, with a young station employee eyeing me suspiciously. But Kimiko did not appear.

When I got back home, I spotted a man standing on the street near my gate. He watched me walk by.

As I passed, he stopped me in a subdued voice. He wore an old overcoat, and had a wispy mustache and sunken cheeks. At a glance, he looked rather like Mr. Hino, who worked the ration desk at the Nigawa town council.

"You're Mr. Durand, right?" the man asked, swaying his flashlight, which shone on the ground. "Where have you been?"

I tried to study his face. "Who are you?" I asked.

"I'm with the police. You know, these days it's a dangerous world even in Nigawa. So we're on the lookout."

"I went to the station to meet my wife."

"Your wife? Ah, I see. Well your wife has just returned."

Kimiko must have been caught buying food on the sly, I thought. But then I was perplexed, because the man was rather calm, and had a hangdog sort of smile on his lips.

"Oh, you brought her back? I was waiting for her at the station—"

"No, this isn't about your wife. It's about you. We often receive letters of complaint about you. They say the congregation doesn't have a high opinion of you. Is that right?" The man held a cigarette in his mouth and struck a match. The flame revealed a scar on his cheek. "I heard you've met McGinn, the Englishman, many times at the Oriental Hotel."

"McGinn?" I asked. "I only met him twice. I have nothing to do with him."

"Well, whatever you say. I'll be back when I have more time to talk to you."

I stood there, stunned, after the man left. Who wrote to the police? And what was this about McGinn?

Then I remembered hearing news about a month ago that McGinn and other prisoners detained in the camp in Takatsuki had been transferred to Osaka. At the time, I received the news without concern. But now I'm convinced that the Japanese police used these prisoners to trump up some evidence to oppress us all.

I opened the door with a shaky hand. Kimiko was crouched there, wordless. Her stiff rucksack lay on the earthen floor.

"Did you see a suspicious man?" I asked.

"No." She shook her head slightly, gazing at me with a blank look in her eyes, the look she had worn on that night. Out of the blue, it hit me that the man might be the detective Ayako-san had been gossiping about. An intense pain shot through my weakened heart.

Kimiko was staring dully at a spot on the tatami mat, holding her legs in her arms under the lamp with its blackout curtain attached. It seemed as if her body was frozen in that posture, fixed. *Were it not for this woman—were it not for this woman...* A voice was murmuring somewhere in my mind. I went back to my room and looked for the strongbox.

Oddly enough, it was not on the desk, where I always kept it, but on the chair with its lid open. The gun was still there. But unmistakably somebody had entered the room while I was away, and rifled through my strongbox.

"Kimiko-san, did you touch this?" I asked, my voice trembling.

Kimiko did not answer, but instead kept repeating that Japanese mantra, in a monotonous tone.

# Chapter III

I pressed the doorbell, but nobody came. Nothing more than the eddying rustle of winds issued from behind the gate. I knew the detective was still watching me. So I kept pressing the bell, without lifting my finger. And then, like a shot, it dawned on me, *Isn't he spying on Mr. Durand?*

"Who's there? Father Breau?" A woman's feeble voice spoke your name through the dark glass door.

"It's me. Chiba." I feigned a cheerful tone, not for her but for the plainclothes man. I tried not to make him suspicious—a tactic which would, incidentally, by no means disadvantage Mr. Durand.

"Chiba-san? Which Chiba-san?"

"Chiba from the church."

Candlelight flickered. The shadow of a middle-aged woman swayed on the wall. She wore soiled clothes and a pair of work pants. She pressed her face into the glass and looked at me dubiously. The light of the candle she held cast unsightly dark circles about her eye sockets.

"So you are from the church." With that, her face grew contorted and quite ugly. "My husband is asleep."

"Ma'am, I just saw a suspicious man."

The candle was extinguished.

"Where is he? Are you sure?" It was Mr. Durand, speaking in a cracked voice.

"He's behind the gate, Mr. Durand."

Immediately they lit a lamp with a blackout curtain,

and there followed a shuffling noise, as if they were hiding something. Without warning, a sickening odor offended my nose. It was not the smell that old, rotting houses have. It was an odor I had never smelled before.

"Where was the detective? Please tell me. Where was he?"

Mr. Durand's face was distorted with terror. Restlessly, his eyes darted between me and a window off to the side; he was covering his mouth with a handkerchief that had brownish stains. His chilblained fingers were misshapen, swollen and purple. And they quivered constantly, because of his alcoholism, I suppose.

"He's at the gate. He said he's from the Nishinomiya police."

Without so much as a word, the old man crawled to the door on his hands and knees, like a dog, and pressed his face against the glass to look out around his house. The pine grove rustled in the wind, deepening the darkness and the chill. The old man's leg peeked out from beneath the frayed hem of his robe, looking rather like a chicken's leg, with the bone visible.

*This man used to be a priest, even if only once. He used to be the man who turned wine into the blood of Christ at the altar, and forgave the people their sins.*

Father, at this moment, and at this moment only, I felt a strong aversion. Not only to Mr. Durand, but to God. I mean, if God really exists, why had He toyed with this Judas—with this hideous old man who now groveled about, utterly terrified—by putting him in a position to accommodate the pain, and the grief, of other people?

"Was it a detective? Not the—how do you say it in Japanese?—*police militaire?*"

Each time the winds rattled the windowpane, he startled at the noise.

"What if they've really come? That's a problem. No, they can't take me away. You know, I'm not alone. I have Kimiko."

I tried to picture the old man as the priest I had never seen. He is reading the mass, wearing his crimson red cassock. I mean that burning, scarlet color that symbolizes the blood the martyrs shed as they were tortured for Christ and for the church. In the valley of death and moaning, Mr. Durand must have, if only for a moment, commended the afflictions of every human being to the cross.

*I'm an old man. Please spare me.*

I felt an impulse to bully the old man, as I did so long ago.

"Mr. Durand," I said. "Unless you've really done something that would create suspicion, the police won't go so far as to torture you."

"Suspicion? I haven't done anything."

"Well, then, you don't have anything to worry about."

"Oh, yes I do. The Japanese police won't believe what I tell them. They ransacked the house just three days ago."

Then, as if asking for a witness, Mr. Durand looked back at the woman, who sat in the corner of the room. She had been gazing at a tear in the tatami mat, without uttering a single word. As she sat there, her shadow looked as if it had been frozen on the wall, forever.

"That's nonsense," I said, curling my lips. "Without a search warrant?"

"We weren't at home. Gone looking for food in Arima. When I returned, I knew it at once. They were careful not to disturb things, so that we wouldn't notice. But Kimiko and I knew immediately."

"Are you sure they were detectives? Everybody in Nigawa is scrounging for food these days."

"It wasn't about food."

"But even if they searched your house, if you haven't done anything—"

The old man shook his head, pressing his fists hard to his temples. And then he looked coldly into my face.

"Are you really a member of the church?"

"Don't you remember?" I poked out my face. "I'm the son of the Chibas. You baptized me when I was a baby."

"Ah!" Mr. Durand was trying in vain to retrieve from his old memories one of the infants whom he had sprinkled with holy water. He moved his bearded mouth slightly and muttered something. "I remember your mother and your aunt. It was a long time ago."

The old man covered my hand with his warm, flabby one, and—who knows what he was thinking—drew in closer to me.

"The strongbox was open," he said in a mutter, as if talking to himself. His breath smelled of fever. "They checked the pistol I had there. They didn't touch our rice or our clothes."

"Pistol?"

"I'm not entirely blameless, I know. Father Breau left the pistol with me some time ago. He'd needed one when he lived in Indochina, you know."

"Father Breau left a pistol with Mr. Durand?" Instinctively, I turned to Kimiko. She seemed to shiver for a second. Then she fixed her eyes again on the tatami mat, with a look somewhere between hatred and fury.

"Do you understand?" Mr. Durand continued. "He asked me to keep it. The military police came around the

103

church so frequently that it had gotten to be annoying. Understand?"

"But why on earth did you agree to keep such a thing?"

"He gives me money every month. You do know my situation, don't you?"

⚬ ◇ ⚬

When I stepped out of the old man's house, a black wind scoured my face. I inhaled, as if gasping, simply because I wanted to purge myself of the odor of that house. Father, that sickening odor in Mr. Durand's house was not that of a rotting old house. If what you call "sin" has a smell—if hatred, jealousy, and curses have a smell—then that must have been the odor of it all. The feverish scent of his breath at my ear lingered.

Yes, I did wonder whether or not I should visit you at the church and tell you everything about the previous night. I don't know to what extent I should believe Mr. Durand's story. But suppose it is true. Then he certainly gave up your secret very easily, and to a person he had practically never met. If he were interrogated by the special political police from Nishinomiya, or by the military police from Kobe, surely this apostate would cough up everything he knows to protect himself. That much was clear to me. But I didn't go to your church. *It doesn't have to be today*, I thought. *I'm tired.* And I rolled onto the bed, looking at the dreary yard lit by the weak sunlight, where some dirty snow still remained under the hedge, frozen. Then the next day came. And I thought, *Why not visit him tomorrow? The plainclothes police won't have come yet.*

Outside the window, the wind was gray just as it had been on that evening when I pressed a kiss on Itoko's lips.

104

Time out of mind, the winds have rattled windowpanes with the same disconsolate rattles, and so will they always. I closed my eyes. An image rose before my mind, in dull hues: Brown gusts of sand rolled up over a stretch of the burnt-out ruins of Tokyo, disappeared, and then rolled up again. Little by little, I managed to ease the matter of Mr. Durand, and also the question of your fate, out of my mind, and to let them be buried by the sands. *When I don't care what will become of myself anymore*, I heard a whisper deep in my mind, *why should I be concerned about Durand and Breau? Sooner or later, what must be simply will be.*

Itoko comes back from the Kawanishi Factory every Sunday evening, as if it were her eternal lot. I don't think she loves me anymore. Nevertheless, she still allows me to bed her down, painfully closing her eyes to bear it, as if she were fulfilling some idle duty, or yielding herself up to fate.

I go to the hospital in Kotoen on Wednesdays and Fridays. It's a small sanatorium that my uncle, a specialist in tuberculosis, built a long time ago. Only the sickest patients are admitted. They lie motionless on their backs, several of them to a room that hasn't been properly taken care of for quite a while. The windowpanes are broken here and there. It was clear at once, even for a mere medical student like me, that most of the patients would waste away to death within a year or so. Proper nutrition is essential for tuberculosis patients, and this they cannot get on meager rations of flour and the occasional pat of butter. Attending to the medical charts with my uncle as he mechanically performed the chest percussions, I noticed that the patients often turned their dark, sallow faces toward the yard, their feverish, languid eyes fixed on a Chinese parasol tree with dead leaves, just outside the window. Their posture and their gaze reminded me of Itoko in the twilight, casting her dark, cold eyes out into the desolate winter yard as I made love to her. They also reminded me of my disease.

I do not know if this deep fatigue was occasioned merely by the war and my illness, or whether it reflects my essential constitution. But, looking back, it seems to me now that it was, after all, this everlasting fatigue that made me retreat from your Catholicism, even before I knew I was doing it. You are a white man: you live in order to ascertain whether or not God exists, and to struggle with sin, and to challenge death. Father, you would often say to the congregation, "The soul is a battlefield. And the Catholic Church is a moving, vital church." But I no longer felt passion for anything, and did not wish to move.

One day, on my way to the hospital, I passed the pine grove behind Mr. Durand's house. Apparently an air-raid warning had just been issued, but, as was my habit, I carried neither a steel helmet nor an air-raid hood.

I heard a sharp sound somewhere, a scraping, metallic *bang*. Looking up, I saw an enemy aircraft flying off at full tilt in the gray skies along the side of Mt. Kabutoyama.

"They've begun to scout out the Kawanishi Factory," I thought. I stood there for a while looking for a trace of the plane that had disappeared behind the mountain. It was a dead afternoon. Not a single sound emanated from the anti-aircraft guns. "Before long, B29s will appear over Nigawa," I said to myself. "It seems inevitable."

Suddenly I heard an intense roar—as if a train were passing overhead. The dead leaves in the coppice rattled. No sooner had I hit the ground than the shadow of what looked like the wings of a huge bird brushed over the street. As I fell, I threw myself into one of the ancient tombs that lay nearby, looking like air-raid shelters. Again, the shadow of the wings swept over the street. I had not heard the guns, but it was clear that a Grumman fighter was going for me.

The thought of death flitted through my mind. But in that ancient tomb, with its odor of rotting earth, death seemed, to me, to be merely the natural course of events. And the only thing that disturbed this luscious death was the maneuvers of the Grumman, and the peal of its engine.

# Chapter IV

## DURAND'S DIARY
### *DECEMBER 15TH*

Here it is, ten days till Christmas, and I had hardly realized.

I remember the Christmases I spent in Lyon, as a child, and later as a seminarian. Candles were lit all over the town. The restaurants, displaying huge, steaming roast turkeys in their windows, were all decorated with colorful lanterns, which reflected and glinted on the blue surface of the Rhone. Each store sparkled with decorations of its own. Shoppers swarmed about, hunting for Christmas gifts. Somewhere, firecrackers popped. The gleeful laughter of young girls echoed. At midnight, Saint Jean Cathedral would ring its bells. And with that as their cue, all the bells in Lyon, including the ones at Saint Bernard, at Saint Bonaventure, and at Saint Francis, leapt in joy and broke out in hosannas that soared through the twinkling night skies until they reached the Fourviere Hills.

*Bon Noël! Bon Noël!* At street corners, outside churches—everywhere people clapped their hands, kissed each other...It was a long time ago. Such a long time. To those who have ever betrayed Him, God will not offer the merest blessing or shred of hope. The joy of Christmas is denied me. God will torment a sinner in hell not simply for a thousand years, or even ten thousand. The damned suffer the fires of hell forever. I cried out loud. I thought I had gone insane. I looked back and saw Kimiko gazing at me, standing at the threshold of the kitchen. When I saw her animal-like, hollow, emotionless look, somehow I felt an intense hatred toward her, and I struck her face. But, falling down on tatami, still she gazed up at me with that empty, impassive look.

## DECEMBER 16TH

"Depart from me, ye cursed, into everlasting fire, prepared for the devil and his angels. Judas cast down the pieces of silver in the temple, and departed, and went and hanged himself."

Tonight I heard footsteps outside the house again. It was a long time before they vanished.

## DECEMBER 17TH

*Departed, and went and hanged himself.*

Why don't I hang myself, like Judas? It would be easy enough to do it. But if God harries those who betray him, even beyond the grave, I prefer to go on living this life of humiliation. I know, better than anyone else could know, how desperately I cling to life—how *base* I am. The footsteps I heard last night were not really those of the Japanese military police, or of a detective. They were echoes of my terror of hell.

Mentioning the detective reminds me of another incident tonight that frightened me. After finishing our scanty meal (three potatoes that Kimiko bought in Arima) Kimiko and I sat at the Japanese *kotatsu*, facing each other in silence. I can't tell what she is thinking. I strike her, I lash out at her, but she just endures the abuse without a word, gazing at me with those vague, long, narrow Oriental eyes. This gaze is not the cold one that a white woman wears when her love has diminished. I can't put my finger on it, but there seems to be some glow of apathy in her eyes that I simply cannot understand.

Tonight I reproached her again. If she really hates me, she should just tell me so, I said. True, her life may have been destroyed. But I lost more, and solely for her sake. And yet she just sits there, silent. If somebody hadn't pressed the doorbell, I might have beaten her again. The bell rang twice, insistently. I turned off the light. In the darkness I hastily groped about for the strongbox where I kept my gun.

But it was a strange student who was talking to Kimiko.

"A detective's out there." He apologized in a lowered voice, panting for breath. "He questioned me. He thought I was peering into your house."

I didn't care about his long-winded excuse. I was far more concerned about the other man, who was still hiding behind the gatepost. But what could I hear, other than the whirlwinds out in the grove, growling like the black ocean?

A glass of wine that Father Breau had given me finally . calmed me down. I took another look at the youth. I remembered seeing that face somewhere, in the distant past. It was just another bland, vacant face of the kind peculiar to Japanese students and intellectuals, complete with a pair of glasses and sunken cheeks.

The eyes of the young man were also small and glassy, like Kimiko's. Staring into his cloudy, lifeless eyes, I was seized by the thought that he could be some minion of the police sent out here to spy on me. Who could say that the Japanese police would not resort to childish tactics like that?

As soon as I saw their trick, a plan formed in my mind. I pretended to be thoroughly frightened so that the young man would hold me in contempt. And then I set out to lay the scene for a "confession" driven by anxiety.

"It was Father Breau who gave me the gun. He bought it in Indochina. I couldn't refuse him because I survive on his charity. I think you understand that, don't you?"

The Japanese words unreeled out of my mouth. I don't know whether or not this man called Chiba is actually a spy. And I don't know how much of my confession he believed. But that's no matter. When I'm arrested some day for possession of that gun, the story might somehow save my life.

After the young man left, my conscience ached. I had betrayed Father Breau. And yet I could not deny that, somewhere in my mind, I felt a sneaking, dark joy for having found a way to survive. I looked back at Kimiko. She was just gazing at me with those dull, emotionless eyes, under the dim light, without uttering a word.

## DECEMBER 18TH

"Why don't you say something?" I shouted, shaking Kimiko's body. "I betrayed Father Breau. Like Judas, I just sold out a man who's taken care of me for eight years. Hate me for it! Why do you look at me like that?" I laughed out loud. And then I saw my face reflected in the mirror.

"I don't care," Kimiko murmured, fixing her hair, which was disheveled from the shaking I gave her. "After all, I'm not a Westerner, and I don't understand this stuff about the church. I'm just a stupid woman. Why can't you just forget about God and the church? Why don't you? You abandoned the church, didn't you? So why are you still obsessed with it? You don't know how much better the Buddha is, who forgives us the minute we say *Namu Amida Buddha*."

I sat up and gaped at Kimiko, in a state of shock. What she had blurted out from sheer spite struck my heart like a sudden revelation.

Eight years ago I betrayed God and left the church, and all the while I've been haunted and gnawed by the nightmare of God's punishment. I hated the church that excommunicated me, and I tried to negate it. Still, I could not forget God, not even for a moment.

But, indeed, if I forgot God, if I liberated myself from Him, there would be no more shuddering—no more terror of death. That had never occurred to me.

It has been twelve years since I started doing missionary work in Japan. And today I understood for the first time the bliss of the heathen (those who do not know God). I don't know if it is truly "bliss." But now at least I think I understand the secret of those eyes of Kimiko and Chiba—the cloudy, long, narrow eyes peculiar to the yellow man. Those eyes, with their dull luster, remind me of the eyes of a dead bird. There is something apathetic and inanimate in their glassy stare that we Westerners find almost uncanny. Theirs are the eyes of a people indifferent to God and to sin and impassive in the face of death. That mantra "Namu Amida Buddha," which Kimiko sometimes recites, is not in the least like our prayers, but a spell, a convenience, for those insensible to sin.

I gazed vacantly at the leaden winter sky for a while, pressing my forehead to the window. It was a heavy sky, so heavy that I couldn't tell whether there was any sun in it or not. It was a Japanese sky.

I might have been saved today, but by a heathen route

utterly abhorrent to the white culture that formed me. I realized, as if for the first time, that if only I could possess those glassy, lifeless eyes, if only I could gradually let go of God, and sin again and again, then someday I, too, would be indifferent to death and sin.

## DECEMBER 20TH

Breau conducts mass at the church between 6:30 and 7:30. That's when I have to steal into the vicarage, and plant the gun somewhere in his study.

I know every nook and cranny of that vicarage, since I lived there myself eight years ago. The vestibule leads to a hallway. Off the hallway to the right is the parlor. And next to that is Breau's study. The only problem is that if I make even a slight noise in that study, someone might get suspicious and open the door.

When I got to the church, the mass was being recited, as usual, in darkness, save for the weak illumination of the milky stained glass. Because of the blackout, they could not turn on the lights. With only two candles burning at the altar, Breau took wine from the acolyte and poured it into the chalice. As always, the congregation consisted of Ayako-san, Miss Ishida, and a few pious, obstinate old women, kneeling and rubbing their palms together.

I stumbled on purpose as I entered the church. The sound echoed loudly in the hollow building. Ayako-san looked back at me from her pew, and stared maliciously under her spectacles. Then she bent over the missal again. *They would all think I was standing behind the pillar like an outcast, during the whole mass.*

I eased back toward the entrance, step by step. Anyhow, I had an alibi now. The cold air of dawn pricked

113

my flushed cheeks. A dog howled somewhere. I looked up to the sky and noticed a few stars still twinkling, faintly.

Through the window, I saw a dim light in the vicarage. The housekeeper seemed to be at work. I could hear the water running.

No lights were on in the vestibule or in the hallway. I removed my shoes in a hurry and felt my way down the dark hallway, on tiptoes. When I reached the parlor I could hear the housekeeper setting the table in the dining room, murmuring to herself. I held my breath and waited for her to go back to the kitchen. I needed to be quick. Holy Communion should begin soon. And Breau wouldn't say the benediction, as it was not Friday. That would leave me a scant ten minutes before he returned to the vicarage.

I proceeded to the study at a dash and tried the door-knob. My knees knocked together. Breau had locked the door! Still worse, I could hear the housekeeper working in the dining room again. If she stepped out into the hallway, she would inevitably see me. I clenched my teeth, then I remembered, out of the distant past, that there was another door, between the parlor and the study.

When I entered the study, I leaned against the wall and tried to catch my breath. Then I pulled myself together and, from the pocket of my overcoat, took out the Browning, which was wrapped in a handkerchief.

The window was growing lighter. Out in the back yard, a small area around the statue of the Virgin Mary of Lourdes was somewhat grayish. The bell rang at the church, announcing the end of mass.

My flashlight revealed, on the large desk, a crude crucifix together with a copy of the *Brunschvicg* edition of *Les Pensées*. The book lay open. Several phrases from the section titled "The Mystery of Jesus" had been underlined, offhandedly, in red pencil.

*Jesus is alone on the earth.*

*Jesus does not regard in Judas his enmity, but the order of God, which He loves and admits, since He calls him friend.*

*Jesus will be in agony even to the end of the world. We must not sleep during that time.*

The drawers were all locked. The glass doors of the bookcase behind me were also tightly shut. But as I pulled the knob again with all my strength, frantic, the door creaked open. Inside were an account book with a black binding, a directory of church members, several card boxes and the like, all neatly lined up, which was just like Breau.

I placed the gun behind those documents, keeping it wrapped in the handkerchief so as not to leave a fingerprint. Then I pulled out the handkerchief.

I slipped out of the study and walked down the hallway. I don't believe the housekeeper saw me. But as I stepped outside, where the light of day was gathering, I was left thunderstruck, as I realized that I had forgotten to shut the glass doors of the bookcase.

# Chapter V

So, if you read this diary, Father Breau, you will see that Mr. Durand planted the gun in your vicarage on the morning of the twentieth. That same afternoon, the old man came out to my house. The reason I know it was the same day is that one of the critically ill patients at the hospital died on the twentieth, and I recall writing out the death certificate for my uncle.

The deceased man, I had heard, was a young student at Kobe College of Commerce, who had been in the hospital, bedridden, for three years. The bacteria had already infiltrated the larynx, so there was nothing my uncle could do except administer calcium injections. Beyond that, he just instructed the man to lie quietly in bed. The X-rays showed two big cavities, right and left, plus a number of tiny exacerbations scattered everywhere.

Still, the patient lingered on. When he strained himself, he ran a fever. But otherwise he chatted with the nurses, in the low, hoarse voice particular to patients with laryngeal tuberculosis, or else he entered something in his notebook, lying in bed.

"Maybe I'll live another two years or so. Don't you think?" Half in jest, half in self-derision, the young man would say some such thing to my uncle or to me as we made the morning rounds. "But, you know, I'd be drafted if I was healthy, and killed in the war. So I wouldn't live long, either way."

On the morning of the nineteenth, the patient fell totally silent. He lay motionless in his bed, agony on his face. *He's dying.* After performing a chest percussion, my uncle looked at me morosely. "I hear that his parents have evacuated. You can wire them, and let them know about this," my uncle said to a nurse in a businesslike manner out in the hallway, and left. I went back to the sickroom that evening. The patient lay there, still in the same posture. He opened his whitish eyes languidly and looked at me, and then he closed them again. The weak sunlight of dusk streamed in aslant from the window, blotting the floor with several pale circles. I felt his forehead. He didn't have a fever.

I sat by the bed for quite a while. And as I looked down at the man's meager body, as he breathed faintly, his thin neck and large head resting on an ice pillow, I remembered having seen a figure very like this.

It was the emaciated old man who starved to death in the midst of the rubble.

Night arrived. I wrapped the patient's legs in a blanket and took his pulse, holding his wrist, which was just skin and bones. I might have had to call my uncle and the nurse.

The young man's pulse was plainly arrhythmic. One moment I felt it faintly on my fingertips, and the next moment it was gone. At still another moment I detected a few weak pulses again.

The button for the bell was right in front of me. I knew that if I pressed it the nurse and my uncle would rush in with a last shot of camphor and some oxygen. But I just stared vacantly at the pale blue button, holding the patient's wrist in my left hand. All I needed to do was stretch my arm out a little. But, somehow, I did not want to move. It wasn't just physical fatigue. Something as heavy as lead was holding down my arm, leaving me too enervated even to press a

117

button. *Dying*. The pulse stopped, then beat faintly again. *Like the old man near the station, this young man is going to die.* Brown gusts of sand rolled up over the burnt-out ruins of Tokyo, disappeared, and then rolled up again—such a scene as that came to mind.

I went home the next afternoon, exhausted. I lay on the bed and thought about the young patient. Soiled remnants of the snow still lay in the yard. The wind rattled the windows, just as it had yesterday, and the day before yesterday. Mr. Durand came to my house that evening.

He tapped at the window with his fingertips. Through the French windows that separated the porch from my bedroom, I saw an ironic smile amongst his yellowish whiskers.

"I just happened to be in the neighborhood. I don't have many friends, you know." As he spoke he fumbled the squash lying on the porch. "Squash is just about the only food these days, isn't it?"

"Didn't the detective come back today?" I asked glumly. "You were really in a panic the other night."

"Anybody would have been." Mr. Durand shook his head and poked a finger into his pipe. "You would have panicked."

I could almost feel his breath on my ear, and almost smell the nauseating odor of his house.

"But you know, *I* don't keep a gun." I felt a dark impulse welling up, just as I had the other night. I wanted to bully the old man. "I wonder if that gun isn't actually yours."

The smirk disappeared from Mr. Durand's face. He gradually retreated into the darkness toward the back, gripping his pipe.

"But don't you..." He gulped, and then murmured. "Don't you have something to hide from the police, too?"

"What do you mean?"

"You don't go to war. You don't work at a factory. You're just idling away the time in Nigawa. What will the Japanese police *do* with such a man?"

I understood now that Mr. Durand had come to threaten me. I also understood the bargaining point: He wanted to make sure I didn't tell you, Father Breau, about the gun.

"You're here to make a deal?"

"A deal? What deal? But, you did lie to the detective, didn't you? You told him you're taking French lessons from me. Well, I guess I can prove you're a liar if I'm interrogated by the police." He laughed out loud, gleefully.

"But if you do want to make a deal, then sell me this squash. Kimiko's struggling to keep food on the table." Flinging this at me, Mr. Durand turned his back and disappeared into the darkness.

Of course, Mr. Durand's threats amount to nothing. He didn't know about my illness. All the same, I became even less motivated to tell you about the gun. No matter how trivial it seems, I just didn't want to get caught up in anything troublesome.

"Saeki's coming back from Himeji for Christmas, but only for a day. Then, it seems, he's going to be shipped off to Kyushu." Itoko was telling me about her fiancé. It was Sunday, two days before Christmas. "He says nothing, but I'm certain he's to be sent on a special attack mission. From what I hear that's what happens to student reserve officers who go to Kagoshima."

Pulling on her gloves, Itoko leaned against the wall, as if all her strength was gone.

"But," I said, nodding, "surely everybody there won't become a kamikaze, right?"

Itoko shook her head. "Oh, yes they will. I know it." I gazed blankly at her, as tears streamed from her wide-open eyes and ran down on her cheeks.

"You still love him."

"I don't know. I don't know who I love any more, or what it means to love somebody."

*That's true—*

Still, I brought my face to Itoko's as we stood there on the porch. Her tears dried, and her face lost its outline in the evening haze; it was just there, ambiguous. I kissed her. It was like pressing my lips to a lukewarm rock, on which a weak sun shines.

"Christmas is the day after tomorrow?"

"That's right. I wonder what they're doing at St. Mary's Women's School."

I walked Itoko to the station on the Hankyu line, as I always did. I was so disgusted with Mr. Durand that, on my way home, I didn't head toward the pine grove. Instead, I walked along the chilly path off the back of your church.

Saeki was coming back on Christmas night. He would spend a day here with Itoko, and then head off to Kyushu to fly a special attack mission. And I made love to Itoko, knowing all of this.

Father, I felt a little pain in my heart, for the first time. It was nothing intense, nothing like the pang of conscience or the terror of sin. I believe it was fundamentally different from that. It was like the faint pain, for example, that you might feel if the tip of a needle pricked your heart.

Come to think of it, I returned to Nigawa in order *not*

to move—in order to be inert. Nevertheless, like the stream that wears down the rocks, already I have shaped the lives of several people, and all in the less than two months I've been back. Saeki is one. The young man who died at the hospital three days ago is another. He would have died anyway. But if I had pressed the button for the bell, and had given him a shot of camphor, he might have lived half an hour longer. You might in any case have been arrested. But if I had told you about Mr. Durand's gun, you'd not have been sent off to the military police in Takatsuki. I thought about karma. A man can just lie in bed, like a patient with a lung disease, and still he sends out ripples around him. It is a weird, strange fact. But how can I remove these fetters now?

When I reached the front of the church, I leaned against the coarse cement wall for a while, my eyes closed. You might be in there, I thought. I will tell you about the gun, just as the parishioners confess their sins on Christmas Eve. This was the first time in two months that I had formed the intention to *move*.

The door of the church creaked dully as I opened it. A red sanctuary lamp was lit in the milk-colored chancel. You were not there. A female student in work pants, her hair done up in a bun, was making her way out, folding a white veil.

"Where is Father Breau?"

"Father Breau?" She replied, eyeing me suspiciously. "He's gone to Takarazuka."

A deep sigh issued from my mouth. *It doesn't have to be tonight.* That tired voice echoed in my mind, in whispers. *I can always come back tomorrow.*

A painting of the Virgin Mary hung in a corner of the chancel. The woman approached it, lit a small candle, and crossed herself.

It is probably a copy of a painting by some old Western

painter, which you had sent for. The woman in the picture is wearing blue clothes. She tilts her head and looks up at the sky with innocent eyes, a rose in her hand.

Somehow, Itoko's face came to mind—her flat, impassive face, the face to which I had brought my own just minutes ago, as we stood on the porch in the evening haze. It was the ambiguous face of a Japanese woman who could never be the model for a painting of the Virgin Mary.

# Chapter VI

## DURAND'S DIARY

### DECEMBER 21ST

I need to calm down. I need to think. Did I or did I not close the glass door of the bookcase in Breau's study?

An account book with a black binding, and a directory of the church members were in the case. I put the gun behind them with the handkerchief. Then I pulled out the handkerchief. That's all I can say for sure.

After that, I don't remember much more than tiptoeing off in a trance from the study to the parlor to the hallway. It is possible that I closed the glass door. I make a futile effort to believe that something like the force of habit caused me to close it. If the door is open when Father Breau returns to the study, however, inevitably he'll be suspicious. And then he'll find the gun behind the directory and the account book.

Never have I cursed my dull, aging brain as I have today! Why on earth did I choose that bookcase out of all the other places? A priest has to consult the account book and the directory on a daily basis. In short, I hid the gun precisely where it was most likely to be discovered.

My only hope is that Father Breau won't know the gun belongs to me. But in any case, if he finds a gun he doesn't own, surely he will call the police.

I imagined all the possible scenarios, one after another. But every one led to the same, dark prospect. I had dug my own grave.

By the way, I visited the youth, named Chiba, yesterday afternoon.

Obviously, he doesn't believe me at all.

## DECEMBER 22ND

I stared into Kimiko's eyes. Instantly, the incident eight years ago came vividly back to mind. That night, Kimiko just gazed up at me with the same blank expression, like a Noh mask. And I slipped into a bottomless morass of lust...

Needless to say, Kimiko knows nothing about the morning of the twentieth. She did not tempt me to the sin with a whisper, as Eve had done with Adam. She was just sitting there on the worn-out tatami mat, Japanese-style. But I felt as if her eyes were permanently frozen there, luring me on to yet another evil.

*You've gotten to the point where it hardly matters how many sins you commit. Why don't you sin and sin again, until the weight of it all wears out your soul? Then you will be as indifferent to death and sin as we yellow people are.*

*But what should I do in the meantime? I ask.*

*Send a letter to the police. Tell them Breau is hiding a gun. That will knock the wind out of his sails. Cut out each letter from the newspaper and glue them to a sheet of paper; that way nobody will recognize your handwriting...*

I cut up the newspaper that afternoon to make the letter to inform the police. I tossed it into the postbox by Nigawa Bridge.

## DECEMBER 23RD

Breau didn't emerge from the church for a long time, which was unusual. At first, I wondered if he had begun to say the benediction after he read the mass. A few congregants paused for their customary idle chat in front of the gate, with Ayako-san and Miss Ishida in the center. After they dispersed, I slipped in the building and peered into the chancel.

Breau lay prostrate on the floor, as priests do during the ritual of ordination. For quite some time he didn't stir, keeping deathly still. And I didn't miss it when he stretched out his arms and grabbed his hair, writhing. It seemed like he was crying. I couldn't imagine why.

As he stood up and went into the sacristy, I scurried outside and approached the front of the vicarage.

Breau stared at me with his childlike blue eyes, as usual. I detected no change in his expression or in his manner. But I clearly recognized the traces of tears.

"What's up, Pierre?"

I mumbled that I had run out of food and had no money to buy more, looking down as if embarrassed.

"Well, why don't you come in, anyway," said Breau, "though I don't have very much on hand."

On entering the study, I cast a quick glance at the bookcase. The glass doors were closed tightly, as they had been on the morning of the twentieth.

"Is the congregation growing?"

"No, it's not," Breau replied, shrugging his shoulders sadly. "I haven't christened anyone for the past two months. And more and more members are skipping mass."

"Isn't it that, after all, there was something wrong in the approach you took to missionary work?"

125

I gradually drew closer to the bookcase, in a casual manner, my pipe in my mouth.

"The approach?"

"Yes. I say so because I've been there. I think you European priests don't really understand the Japanese. In Europe the Christian Church has a long tradition, whereas in Japan there is none whatsoever, and yet you think about the Japanese in essentially the same way. What I'm saying is that you all assume that the church can simply send a priest to Japan just as it might send one to Landes. Isn't that right? The approach to missionary work is uniform—formulaic. Well, just picture a perfectly ordinary Japanese person, for example. Do you think he really *needs* the Lord? Do you suppose Christ seems real to him?"

Inside, the bookcase was just as it had been that morning. The account book, the directory, and all the card boxes were in their places. It looked like they hadn't been touched.

"You say a very strange thing, indeed," cried Breau, indignant. "Catholicism transcends all races, and embraces everyone."

"Except for apostates like me."

For the first time, I felt a kind of superiority over him. "Breau," I said to him in my mind, "do you really think your God will take root into this damp country among its yellow people? You don't notice that yellow men have eyes like Kimiko's and that young man Chiba's. You're ignorant because you've never really been tainted by their sins, have never really soiled your white hands. But I found the secret of their soul when I forced myself on Kimiko..."

"You are right," I continued, "but still you forget that the Japanese have never had one God, though they've certainly had gods."

"Those gods will be conquered, Pierre. Catholicism

will take up their heretical pantheism and, as in the Miracle of Cana..."

I had no reason to stay, now that I'd seen what I'd come to see. A smirk appeared on my lips.

Breau came along to see me off at the door, as he always did.

"Don't worry," he whispered abruptly, slipping some money into my hand. "And forget everything."

"Forget what?" I looked vacantly at his smile.

"After all, Pierre, Catholicism *is* the Miracle of Cana. And what made you try to kill yourself will vanish, today and forever."

His voice was so clear and soft that I almost believed he was still on his previous subject.

"Goodbye, Pierre. And merry Christmas!"

Father Breau gripped my hand again, and disappeared into the parlor.

As I walked to Nigawa Bridge, I thought about Breau's strange words. At first I couldn't figure out what he meant.

The winds were blowing down hard from Mt. Kabutoyama, as always. I covered my face with my hands to block out the wind, and again I had a vision of myself in death. It was utterly unlike what I had seen in the darkness the other day, the day I started this diary. It had happened at this very Nigawa Bridge on my way home from mass, when I covered my face with my hands as the icy wind off the mountain hit it right on. That time, the image was of my face at the moment of my death. But the image invoked this time was of myself in hell, exactly as the Book of Revelation describes it. I saw the angels pouring out seven vials over the earth, and I saw the dead (and how many of them there were!) raise their arms, cry, gnaw at their tongues, and curse God as they were borne away in the muddy waters. And appearing and disappearing among the faces was the face of this man Durand.

Of course, it all happened in a moment. When I opened my eyes, a young man passed by me on a bicycle, shouting, "What the heck are you doing!? Don't stand in the middle of the bridge!" Black smoke rose from the chimney of the Kawanishi Factory, and streamed away in the leaden sky. A siren echoed. Students of Kansei Gakuin, wearing puttees, rambled along the riverbank, carrying gunnysacks. Everything looked as it had yesterday morning, or the morning of the day before yesterday, or the morning of someday half a year ago. I'm still alive, and these Japanese are still alive. Yet, while I reject God, I can never deny His existence. I'm imbued with Him to the tips of my fingers. And here these students, the young man who bumped into me as he passed by, Chiba and Kimiko—all these Japanese can get along fine without God. They are able to live in ambiguity, in perfect indifference to the church, to the pain of sin, and to the desire for salvation—to everything we whites believe to be essential to human beings. Why is it? Why?

Leaning against the railing, I raised my hands before my eyes. They were chilblained and swollen, with purple blemishes. But these hands with blond hair on the back were unmistakably those of a white man, those of a man who had to choose either to believe in God or to hate him. I can't become yellow. I can't change the color of my skin.

I remembered, vaguely—in the same way one might look at a rainy scene and imagine what it would be like if it were sunny—that the day after tomorrow was Christmas.

# Chapter VII

Father, you said to Mr. Durand that Catholicism was like the Miracle of Cana. And I remember, when I was a child, I was taught that Christ's first miracle was to turn water into wine. I was also taught that Divine providence is at work behind the fate of all men, and that, just as if it were changing water into wine, it can purify every sin through grace. But what you call "providence" merely seems to me to be the fate that cannot be changed.

What would have happened if I had sat down and remained in the church to wait for you on that night, the day before yesterday? Or it needn't even have been the day before yesterday. How about this morning? If I had visited the vicarage just two hours earlier and told you what Mr. Durand had said, you might never have been sent to Takatsuki. But I am more inclined to think that everything would have been the same, sooner or later. Probably this was simply your fate, which is beyond both Mr. Durand's scheme and my laziness, and you had to face it anyway. I wonder.

When I awoke this morning, my limbs were feverish, as they always are. With a paralyzing fatigue in my every joint, I murmured to myself, *Ah, yes, I really must go see him.* The sputum I coughed up onto a sheet of paper was yellowish and thick. I can tell that each time I make love to Itoko, my illness slightly worsens. *I'll go when I feel refreshed. Most likely the Father will be free around noon, anyway.*

The sky is overcast and leaden. *In a little while, in just a little while, I'll go to the church.* I murmured to myself, as if trying to calm my mind, all the while knowing that I'd never feel refreshed, and that I would never go to the church.

Besides, today is the day Saeki comes back from the air base in Tsu to visit Itoko. Itoko will see him, and Saeki might find out about us. But what can I possibly do? I could accept Saeki's judgment and expiate my sins. But what good would come of a little drama like that? I don't believe for a minute that my relationship with Itoko couldn't have been helped, and I will never chalk it up to the war. But I feel too languid to be ashamed of it, or to suffer.

It was a tranquil afternoon, soundless but for the now-customary buzzer going off to announce another warning out in the shack of our family's old retainer. I slept awhile longer.

I woke up to find Itoko sitting by the bed.

"Didn't you go to meet Saeki?"

"He'll arrive at Sannomiya at four o'clock. But Father Breau—"

She told me that you'd been arrested. Two plainclothes MPs visited the church when you were hearing the Christmas confessions, and carried you away.

"I went there to tell Father Breau about Saeki. And when I entered the gate, he was coming down the stairs, flanked by two MPs. The church members were stunned. But he was smiling at them. It was as if," Itoko's voice was quavering, as might be expected, "as if he already knew his fate."

"What about Mr. Durand?"

Itoko shook her head. *As if he already knew his fate.* That crouching old man I saw by the station in Shinano-machi; Tokyo with brown gusts of sand rolling up and disappearing; the young man who died of tuberculosis in a private room; Itoko's white, pained profile as she gazed at the desolate winter yard: each of these images rose up in my mind and then disappeared in turn, with no particular meaning, and with no particular relation to one another.

Strange to say, the news of your arrest brought no surprise, no emotion. It seemed to me as if everyone and everything was locked into a deep, undeviating track. I took Itoko's hand and tugged at it.

"No," said Itoko, weakly resisting. But her body fell down onto the bed by itself. "No. Not today. Not on the day Saeki comes back."

As if touching my toe to the evening ocean to test the temperature of its lukewarm waters, I abandoned myself to the languid river of lust. At that very moment people were dying, being maimed, groaning. At that very moment, you were being interrogated in some small room. And Itoko and I lay there on the bed, motionless, exhausted, with our eyes staring up at the ceiling.

The buzzer sounded, again and again, making its metallic din. *Enemy aircraft...over Osaka Bay...Kansai Military District Air Defense Headquarters.* I heard a young man's excited, high-pitched voice amongst the buzzing.

"You should take cover in the bomb shelter," the old retainer said, tapping the window with his finger. "Enemy planes are close."

The crack of a distant antiaircraft gun shook the windowpane. *I have to get up,* I muttered. But again that exhausted, listless feeling weighed down my limbs. *It's still a little early to run for the shelter.*

At that moment, I heard a faint noise in the yard. Something wrapped in green paper fell to the ground.

I saw someone hide himself behind the hedge. I thought it was our old man, but then I recognized the worn-out brown overcoat I could just make out through the bushes. It was what Mr. Durand had been wearing when he turned up on the porch on the twentieth, at dusk.

*What did he come here for?*

I left Itoko on the bed and went down to the yard, climbing out the French window. The old fellow noticed me, and walked away, dragging his rheumatic legs, along the road that leads to Nigawa Bridge.

I picked up the package Mr. Durand had dropped. It was a book of some kind, first wrapped in green paper, and, under that, in another layer of paper from a foreign newspaper. I noticed, through the tears in the newspaper, Mr. Durand's handwriting in black ink: "Please give this to Breau, someday."

I was going back into the house, when, all of a sudden, our old retainer shouted. I heard a roar over my head, like a train going by. A tremendous wind hit my face. Roofing tiles showered the ground. Zigzagging cracks tore through the French window I'd left open, and through the walls of the house. It looked like someone had thrown India ink at it. For a moment, I clearly saw the walls shatter into pieces. Intense concussions struck me as I staggered to the ground.

Black smoke from the Kawanishi Factory drifted over the yard. What has to be described as a clamoring whoop, as if a vast crowd of people were crying out all at once, echoed in from the distance, together with the sounds of burning explosions...Pressing my face against the ground, I tried to remember the sweet, sour smell of the ancient tomb.

Then a momentary hush fell. It was almost eerie. Itoko had fallen out of bed and now lay in the midst of the debris torn up by the blast. Fragments of glass, like pearls, fell from her cheeks as I helped her sit up. Red blood trickled down. "At four o'clock," Itoko muttered sleepily, opening her white eyes, "Saeki comes back. I must go." Then she closed her eyes again. "At four o'clock—"

⚬⚬⚬ ◇ ⚬⚬⚬

"A Western fellow is dead here!" Someone was shouting out in the street. I thought, vaguely, that Mr. Durand had died.

The B29s flew over the Kii Peninsula and then disappeared into the ocean, at dusk. Now, the hush is uncanny, so quiet that it's hard to credit the hell on earth that the bombing made only two hours ago. The black flames that licked over the Kawanishi Aircraft Factory are now extinguished, though I can still feel dull bangs through the cracked window, if only faintly, from whatever it is that's exploding...

I wrote this letter by the light of stubby candle. Now it's time for me to put down the pen. It's already midnight. And I had forgotten that it was Christmas. For you, Father Breau, I imagine that this is the night on which God gave Light to all this darkness. But for us yellow men, there is neither darkness nor light, nor any distinction between them. That's what Mr. Durand discovered just before he died. I can still see his back as he walked away, dragging his rheumatic legs, a few seconds before the bombs fell. And it's not the bomb that killed him. I can't help thinking that he killed himself, now that he had handed his diary to me. Maybe he is being judged for that by your God now. Or maybe he is in some yellow world, with no judgment or punishment, where he closes his tired eyes and melts into sleep. I don't know. Still, I feel now that we could understand Mr. Durand, white though he was like you, whereas nothing could be more remote from we yellow men than your pure white world. And that might be the reason I wrote this letter.

## TRANSLATOR'S NOTE:

The English translation of Pascal's *Pensées* quoted above is that of W. F. Trotter.